PHILOSOPHY OF COMPUTING
AND INFORMATION

Other interview books from Automatic Press ◆ ⊻̵P

Formal Philosophy
edited by Vincent F. Hendricks & John Symons
November 2005

Masses of Formal Philosophy
edited by Vincent F. Hendricks & John Symons
October 2006

Political Questions: 5 Questions for Political Philosophers
edited by Morten Ebbe Juul Nielsen
December 2006

Philosophy of Technology: 5 Questions
edited by Jan-Kyrre Berg Olsen & Evan Selinger
February 2007

Game Theory: 5 Questions
edited by Vincent F. Hendricks & Pelle Guldborg Hansen
April 2007

Legal Philosophy: 5 Questions
edited by Morten Ebbe Juul Nielsen
October 2007

Normative Ethics: 5 Questions
edited by Thomas S. Petersen & Jesper Ryberg
November 2007

Philosophy of Mathematics: 5 Questions
edited by Vincent F.Hendricks & Hannes Leitgeb
January 2008

Epistemology: 5 Questions
edited by Vincent F.Hendricks & Duncan Pritchard
September 2008

Complexity: 5 Questions
edited by Carlos Gershenson
September 2008

Probability and Statistics: 5 Questions
edited by Alan Hájek & Vincent F. Hendricks
September 2008

See all published and forthcoming books in the 5 Questions series at
www.vince-inc.com/automatic.html

PHILOSOPHY OF COMPUTING AND INFORMATION

5 QUESTIONS

edited by

Luciano Floridi

Automatic Press ◆ ⟂P

Automatic Press ♦ $\frac{\vee}{\mathsf{I}}$P

Information on this title: www.vince-inc.com/automatic.html

© Automatic Press / VIP 2008

This publication is in copyright. Subject to statuary exception
and to the provisions of relevant collective licensing agreements,
no reproduction of any part may take place without
the written permission of the publisher.

First published 2008

Printed in the United States of America
and the United Kingdom

ISBN-10   87-92130-09-7   paperback
ISBN-13   978-87-92130-09-9   paperback

The publisher has no responsibilities for
the persistence or accuracy of URLs for external or
third party Internet Web sites referred to in this publication
and does not guarantee that any content on such
Web sites is, or will remain, accurate or appropriate.

Typeset in LaTeX2$_\varepsilon$
Cover photo from *U.S. Army Photo*,
graphic design by Vincent F. Hendricks

Contents

ii

Preface

When Vincent F. Hendricks invited me to contribute to, and edit, this volume on the *Philosophy of Computing and Information* (PCI), I was flattered. When I discovered that I had the freedom to invite some of the best researchers in the world to join me in the enterprise, and pick their brainss about their experiences, interests and views, I was thrilled. It was only when I finally realised what it meant to coordinate such an effort that I was overwhelmed by its magnitude. After some thoughts and consultations with several colleagues, I came to the conclusion that it would be impossible to produce the sort of volume that I had initially envisaged, something that would recount personal stories, provide insightful ideas on the past, present and future status of PCI, while also giving an overview of who's who in the field and, to top it all, outline the lines of research that are, or could be, fruitful. As a kid in a toyshop, I had a list of invitees that was far too long, given the size of the planned volume, and far too many questions to ask. I also wished to provide some balance, with views coming not just from philosophy, but also from science and industry. The whole project seemed a recipe for failure. If I have even only partly succeeded in my plan, it is because of Vincent's support, the patience and availability of the contributors, and the extraordinary help of Valeria Giardino, my personal assistant, and Joanna Gillies, my research assistant. They really made the volume feasible.

If I were the reader, I would probably skip this brief introduction and jump to the contribution of my preferred researcher. The book is constituted of independent chapters, which indeed could be read in any order. But if the reader can bear with me for another minute or two, I would like to clarify a couple of points that might enhance the reading experience.

With an analogy, PCI could be compared to a pair of pincers. On the one hand, this relatively new field is concerned with the critical investigation of the conceptual nature and basic principles of information, including its dynamics (especially computation), utilisation (especially in ethically sensitive contexts) and sciences. On the other hand, PCI seeks to elaborate and apply information-theoretic and computational methodologies to classic philosophical problems. The reader will find that the following interviews alternate between these two approaches. Their convergence represents a remarkable strength. A second feature of the volume worth emphasising is that PCI owes much to earlier research in the philosophy of Artificial Intelligence (AI). As the perceptive reader may notice, the latter never acquired all the importance that it deserved, but it paved the way for further studies in PCI, which would otherwise have been unlikely to flourish.

Coming to the structure of the volume, all participants were asked the same set of five questions:

1. Why were you initially drawn to computational and/or informational issues?

2. What example(s) from your work (or the work of others) best illustrates the fruitful use of a computational and/or informational approach for foundational researches and/or applications?

3. What is the proper role of computer science and/or information science in relation to other disciplines?

4. What do you consider the most neglected topics and/or contributions in late 20th century studies of computation and/or information?

5. What are the most important open problems concerning computation and/or information and what are the prospects for progress?

The contributors were invited to write a series of specific answers or use the questions as starting points for longer essays. The authors have taken full advantage of this freedom, and this explains the very different lengths and styles of the contributions.

Finally, it is almost pointless to remind the reader that, nowadays, computing and information, and their philosophy in the broad sense, play a most important scientific, technological and conceptual role in our world. Developments in computer and information science, their techniques and methods, have sparked the formulation of, and the solution to, central problems in endless contexts. Their profound influence on our lives is well captured by the view that ours is a global, trans-national "information society". Computational and information-theoretical insights and technologies have sharpened, radicalized and extended how we conceptualise and deal with reality and our lives. Without the computer/information revolution, our century would be unrecognizable. In short, computer science and information science have continued to serve as a fulcrum in the current development of human history. This book attempts to put together the views and experiences of some of the visionary pioneers and most influential thinkers in such a fundamental area of our intellectual development. I hope you will enjoy it and find it inspiring. It was a difficult editorial project to follow, but, on a personal note, it turned out to be worth all the effort.

Luciano Floridi
Oxford
May 22, 2008

Acknowledgements

I would like to thank Claus Festersen and Rasmus Rendsvig when encountering LaTeX-related problems. Also I would like to thank our publisher Automatic Press ♦ $\frac{\vee}{\mathsf{I}}$P, in particular senior publishing editor V.J. Menshy, for continuing to take on these 'rather unusual academic' projects.

Luciano Floridi
Oxford
May 22, 2008

1

Margaret A. Boden

Research Professor of Cognitive Science

University of Sussex (Centre for Cognitive Science), UK

1. Why were you initially drawn to computational and/or informational issues?

I was converted to computationalism within the space of a few minutes: a Eureka! moment, one might say. It was in September 1962, a couple of days after crossing the pond from England to study psychology with Jerome Bruner at Harvard. Rifling through a box of second-hand books in a bookshop on Massachusetts Avenue, I picked up – by chance – a copy of *Plans and the Structure of Behavior*, by George Miller, Eugene Galanter, and Karl Pribram: MGP, for short (1960). And it changed my life.

MGP's volume was the first to apply a computer-programming approach to the whole of psychology: animal and human, cognitive and emotional/motivational, normal and psychopathological – even including such ambitious topics as personality and hypnosis. It was (inevitably) simplistic and hand-waving, and it was sometimes careless as well. Nevertheless, it was a work of vision. In effect, it was a manifesto for the then-emerging interdisciplinary area of cognitive science. Indeed, I now think that the best way of judging the achievements of cognitive science over the last fifty years is to compare today's work with the hopes and promises expressed by MGP (Boden 2006: 6.iv.c, 17.iv).

Standing there in the bookshop, it was instantly clear to me that it offered a way of asking, and perhaps even answering, questions that had perplexed me ever since I was a schoolgirl. These were the nature and evolution of mind; the mind-body problem in general; and purpose, free will, and psychopathology in particular.

I'd been intrigued, for instance, by paranoia, multiple personality, automatisms, and hypnosis. And I was especially puzzled by psychosomatic phenomena such as hysterical paralyses and anaesthesias, wherein the bodily area bereft of movement or feeling *does not* correspond with any specifiable set of spinal nerves. Here, the mind – that is, the person's *concepts/beliefs*, about what counts as an *arm* for instance (namely, a body-part bounded by the line of a sleeveless shirt) – was seemingly not merely influencing the body, as in normal voluntary action, but even overcoming it. How was that possible? I'd asked myself that question for many years, but with scant profit. Now this little book, I realized, was pointing towards an answer. (Eventually, I would spell it out: Boden 1970.)

There was a reason why I was persuaded by *Plans* so instantaneously – indeed, why I kicked myself for not having had the same idea already. For in the late-1950s, at the other Cambridge, I'd studied philosophy with Margaret Masterman at her pioneering Cambridge Language Research Unit. (I'd also encountered Gordon Pask, who was initiating computer-aided learning devices in a tiny back-room at the Unit.) Masterman was one of the first people in the world to work on machine translation, and on what would now be called AI learning (Masterman 2007). She'd convinced me that computers could help us to clarify the semantic relationships between concepts, and even to disambiguate individual words by using contextual cues (unusually, her machine-translation research used a thesaurus rather than a dictionary). But because she focussed on conceptual structure rather than mental process, and (given the primitive state of computing in the mid-1950s) couldn't do any actual programming, I hadn't realized that her approach might be generalized to the phenomena that most interested me: purpose, freedom, and psychopathology. The missing emphasis on process and on programs, of course, was precisely what MGP were offering in their book.

In a nutshell, they were indicating how AI could help us to understand how purpose (a.k.a. "plans") is possible in a fundamentally mechanistic universe. Already primed by Masterman and Pask, I got the point immediately. I was even more interested in their speculative remarks about personal and clinical psychology than in their more detailed discussions of language, memory, and problem-solving. Very soon, I would apply their ideas to the rich theory of normal and abnormal personality structure developed by William McDougall (Boden 1965, 1972). This theory was an appropriate challenge because McDougall, unlike his contemporary Sigmund Freud, did not believe that mind can be grounded in a purely mechanistic base.

2. What example(s) from your work (or the work of others) best illustrates the fruitful use of a computational and/or informational approach for foundational researches and/or applications?

This question is invidious, of course, because there are so many strong candidates. Moreover, it doesn't distinguish between pioneering but simplistic work (such as MGP's) that has been historically fruitful and work that has actually achieved a convincing theory and/or a useful application. So one's answer will depend very much on one's personal interests, not just one's knowledge of the field. Since my interests are in cognitive science, not in technology, my answers will favour mind-related theories over 'pure' AI applications. (It must be said, however, that some of the most commercially successful applications have decidedly 'impure' origins. Data-mining grew out of Earl Hunt's theory of human concept-learning, for instance – Boden 2006: 13.iii.f. And personal computing, and virtual reality too, grew largely from the 1960s psychological insights of Bruner and Seymour Papert-Boden 2006: 13.v–vi.)

As for my own work, this (as remarked above) has focussed on showing how computational ideas can clarify fundamental – philosophical and psychological – questions about the nature of mind. It has been especially concerned with purpose, personality, and creativity (Boden 1972, 1977/87, 1990/2004). My discussion of creativity, in particular, has influenced a number of AI studies of the field (e.g. Wiggins 2001, Thornton 2005, Copley and Gartland-Jones 2005).

As for the founding fathers, if asked to pick just one I'd choose Marvin Minsky. Not for his technical contribution: there, my vote would go to Allen Newell. Nor for his linking of AI to psychology: there, I'd favour Newell and Herb Simon jointly – and MGP, of course. Rather, for his vision regarding both the potential and the obstacles facing AI. Minsky's "Steps" paper (1956/1961) was a superb early manifesto for AI , not least because it flagged the many difficulties; indeed, it can still be read with profit. More recently, he has applied a wide diversity of AI results, and methodologies, in asking basic questions about the highly complex system that is the human mind – emotions and all (Minsky 1985, 2006).

Singling out just one example from the last fifty years is even more problematic, and even more unfair to the people not named – although that word "foundational" in the question does narrow the field considerably. However, here goes: in my view, the most fruitful use of a computational approach for foundational researches in AI and cognitive science is the work of Aaron Sloman. I say this for three reasons.

First, thanks to his expertise as an analytic philosopher, he has brought AI insights to bear on a wide range of fundamental philosophical questions (Sloman 1978, 1986, 1987) – including, in recent years, the nature of computation as such (2002). Second, he (like Minsky) has long focussed on mental architecture, asking how human and animal minds – and also imaginable but nonexistent types of mind (1978: ch. 6) – are possible. Among the many phenomena that he has illuminated are emotions (even including grief) and consciousness (Sloman 2000, 2001; Sloman and Chrisley 2003; Wright et al. 1996). And third, his work in building AI systems has been imaginative, and largely ahead of its time.

His 1970s POPEYE program (Sloman 1978: ch. 9; cf. Sloman 1983, 1989), for instance, addressed the complexities of vision in light of general architectural principles (clarifying some familiar concepts such as *interest, consciousness,* and *experience* on the way). It was sidelined by the explosion of interest in David Marr's (1979) work, which took a very different approach, but has recently been acknowledged as an inspiration for the 'dual-pathway' theory of vision (Milner and Goodale 1993). Moreover, his group have recently modelled the various types of anxiety besetting a nursemaid caring for several bored, hungry, and sometimes dangerously crawling babies (Wright and Sloman 1997). They have also made the core of this model available for others as a 'test-bed' to use in their own research (Sloman 1995; Sloman and Poli 1995).

3. What is the proper role of computer science and/or information theory in relation to other disciplines, including other philosophical areas?

Computer science – or rather, AI /A-Life – has two great strengths to offer the other disciplines in cognitive science. It can help to clarify theories in philosophy, psychology, linguistics, anthropology, and neuroscience, and in relevant areas of biology too. Even more important, it provides ideas that can be used as substantive theoretical concepts in these disciplines. That's to say that it helps us not only to clarify theories relating to the mind, or mind-brain, but also to *construct* them.

It follows that the relation of AI /A-Life to cognitive science is very different from that of computer science to chemistry (say), or meteorology. No computational chemist believes that the same molecular interactions go on in his computer as in his test-tubes. But cognitive scientists in general do believe that *similar sorts of computational/informational processes* occur in human and animal minds as occur in the machines used to model their theories.

To be sure, those machines, and those processes, are identified differently by different research groups. They include symbolic, connectionist, situated, dynamical, and homeostatic models – not to mention hybrid systems combining two or more approaches. There's no universally accepted theoretical pathway within cognitive science as a whole. Indeed, there's a regrettable hostility between differing approaches – "regrettable", because all of them (and probably more) will be needed to emulate the rich space of possible minds. This hostility originated in the 1950s, when the relatively eclectic cybernetics movement developed a schism between symbolic and connectionist/dynamical work – or, in other words, between studies of *meaning* and of *adaptation* (Boden 2006: 4.ix).

A final word, on the subject of "disciplines": it's often said, not least by computer scientists, that AI itself isn't a discipline (Boden 2006: 13.vii.a). Sometimes, this is a polite way of accusing AI workers of being experimental rather than theoretical in their approach – and often sloppy, too. Other times, it's a way of saying that there's no neat classification of topics that are potential grist for the AI mill. Just about anything, even (as we've seen) creativity and grief, can be studied in AI.

There's some justice in both those claims, even though they're sometimes motivated at least as much by jealousy about funding and publicity as by high intellectual standards. But it's also true that when AI does manage to solve a problem, people tend to locate the answer outside AI as such. (Philosophy often suffers a similar fate, its successes being renamed as "science" or "logic".) Data mining, for instance, is regarded today as straight computer science, even though – as remarked above – it grew out of AI work based in cognitive psychology. Many other examples could be given. In short, having bravely located firm ground in unmapped and marshy territory, AI's successes are renamed "computer science" and what was once exploration becomes tourism.

4. What do you consider the most neglected topics and/or contributions in late 20th century studies of computation and/or information?

Although anthropology took one of the six points on the "Sloan hexagon" when cognitive science was defined for the Alfred P. Sloan Foundation in the late-1970s (n.a. 1978), there has been hardly any computational work on it (Boden 2006: ch. 8). Among the exceptions are a multi-network model of distributed cognition on board ship (Hutchins 1995) and a schema-based connectionist theory of US-American beliefs about marriage (Strauss and Quinn 1997). There are two main reasons for this neglect. One is the counter-cultural, post-modernist, turn in professional anthropology since the 1970s, whereby 'scientific approaches were explicitly discredited. This was an aspect of the "science wars" (which affected psychology also–Boden 2006: 6.i.d), wherein "objectivity" – and "reality" too – was dismissed by philosophical opponents as a self-serving myth (Gross and Levitt 1998). The other is the fact that a host of questions of interest to anthropologists, and raised by anthropologists (such as Jerome Barkow, widely believed to be a psychologist), have been relabelled as "evolutionary psychology".

In addition, anthropological questions are even more complex, and even less suited to computer modelling, than those addressed in psychology. However, they require psychological answers as well as anthropological data. Work on perceptual and aesthetic preferences is needed for comparative aesthetics, for example, and theories of communication, developmental psychology, and hallucination are all important for the anthropology of religion (Boden 2006: 8.ivand vi). In all those cases, the psychological theories concerned involve computational concepts and insights, even though functioning models are thin on the ground.

Another neglected topic is post-1960s Chomskian linguistics. The theories of principles and parameters, or PP (Chomsky and Lasnik 1977), and of minimalism (Chomsky 1995), have been ignored outside professional linguistics. (Even there, many people don't disagree with them so much as deride them – Boden 2006: 9.viii–ix.) Given that the PP theory offers an epigenetic account of language development that might admit of formal study, it's perhaps surprising that cognitive scientists have paid so little attention to it. It's less surprising within AI / NPL, because other accounts of syntax are more computationally tractable (e.g. Gazdar et al. 1985; Pollard and Sag 1994), and because corpus-based (statistical) approaches are becoming evermore popular (Sampson and McCarthy 2004).

5. What are the most important open problems concerning computation and/or information and what are the prospects for progress?

I've recently been rash enough to list the (twenty-seven) state-of-the-art advances in AI and cognitive science that I regard as the most promising (Boden 2006: 17.iii). For the bulk of them, the "prospects for progress" are good. But with respect to what I regard as "the most important open problems", the prospects are less sunny. For these problems are largely philosophical in nature, and – notoriously – philosophical problems don't get solved in a hurry.

One important unsolved problem is the nature of computation as such. It's often assumed, especially by philosophers with no practical experience of AI, that we know what computation is because Alan Turing (with Alonzo Church) told us. Granted, Turing's definition remains the clearest. But AI scientists have long sought to widen our concept of what computation, in practice, is.Brian Smith did this a quarter-century ago when discussing the semantics of programming languages and since then has developed a startlingly unorthodox metaphysical position which assimilates computation to intentionality (Smith 1985, 1996). Smith's account is not to everyone's taste: some regard it as not merely maverick but mad (although others deem it hugely exciting). But the general question he raises is now attracting increasing attention (e.g. Scheutz 2002). This interest is driven only in part by the prospect of different sorts of hardware, such as quantum computers. It's driven also by people's growing experience of what computers, in practice, can do.

Ron Chrisley (2000) has compared computationalism in cognitive science with physicalism. The physicalist doesn't say that everything that exists is covered by our current physics, but by *whatever the best theory of physics turns out to be*; similarly, to regard minds as computational systems is to believe that they can in principle be understood by *whatever the best theory of what computers do turns out to be*. This is helpful – but the fly in the ointment is that there may one day be genuine disagreement as to just what can properly be classed as a "computer".

Another open question concerns the relation between life and mind. This is problematic partly because there's no universally agreed definition of life. Some definitions allow for the possibility of life-in-computers, or "strong" A-Life , whereas others do not (Boden 1999). Even more to the point, the common assumption that life is a necessary precondition of mind is more often stated than argued – and, when argued, isn't argued convincingly (Boden 2006: 16.xi). If it's correct then, in principle, A-Life is a prolegomenon to AI. Indeed, many A-Life workers believe this. But are they right? And if so, why?

Thirdly, there's the problem of the nature and origin of meaning, or intentionality. This is a core problem of philosophy, and has been addressed also by philosophically minded AI / A-Life workers such as Sloman, Smith, Luc Steels (1998), and Ezequiel di Paolo (1998). The huge theoretical differences between the writings of those four men indicate the difficulties, and the immense room for controversy, here.

In professional philosophy, it isn't even agreed that there could in principle be a naturalistic (scientific) theory of intentionality, whether based in computers or in biology and neuroscience. Neo-Kantian, or 'Continental', philosophers in general deny this vociferously (Boden 2006: 16.vi–viii). On their view, intentionality is the precedent and ground of scientific thinking, so can't possibly be explained by science.

My own view is that a naturalistic account must be possible, and that it is most likely to be grounded in evolution and the teleological processes that evolution has begotten (e.g. Millikan 1984). But there are some counterintuitive implications to this view, one of which is that a magically constructed molecule-for-molecule simulacrum of a human being (the so-called "swamp man") would mouth the same words as us but without their having any meaning whatsoever. Perhaps the best way to deal with this objection is to point out that according to thermodynamics there could conceivably be a snowball in hell, if only for a split second – but no physicist stops to worry about it. If imaginary snowballs in hell don't spell rejection for thermodynamics, then the imaginary swamp man needn't spell rejection for evolutionary semantics. Nevertheless, it must be admitted that there's no universally agreed evolutionary semantics, not even among those who are generally sympathetic to such an approach.

Finally, there's the still-open problem of the nature of conscious experience, or qualia. Many problems concerning consciousness have been illuminated, or even solved, by cognitive science – which is to say, by research employing computational concepts of one sort or another. (Examples include the nature of attention and the possibility of mental dissociations, including multiple personality disorder – Boden 2006: 7.i.h–i and 14.x.) But qualia have proven to be more intractable. The most persuasive account I've come across is Sloman's (1996a,b, 1999), wherein the mind is conceptualized as a complex virtual machine implemented in the brain, and qualia are a particular (computational) feature of the relevant virtual architecture. (Daniel Dennett's approach is similar in many ways, but unlike Sloman he *denies* the reality of qualia: Dennett 1988, 2005.)

To say that I find this the most persuasive account isn't to say that I see it as fully persuasive. (The neo-Kantians, of course, reject naturalist theories of consciousness just as they reject naturalist accounts of meaning, and on much the same grounds.) I suspect that a fundamental revolution in our concepts, within both neuroscience and the philosophy of mind, may be needed before we can really understand qualia (Boden 2006: 14.xi.d–e). However, I'm convinced (not being a neo-Kantian) that computational insights, as well as neuroscienti?c findings, will make an essential contribution.

References

n.a. (1978), *Report of the State of the Art Committee to the Advisors of the Alfred P. Sloan Foundation*, October 1, 1978, in F.Machlup and U. Mansfield (eds.), *The Study of Information: Interdisciplinary Messages* (NewYork: Wiley-Interscience), 1983, 75–80.

Boden, M. A. (1965), 'McDougall Revisited', *Journal of Personality*, 33: 1–19.

Boden, M.A. (1970), 'Intentionality and Physical Systems', *Philosophy of Science*, 37: 200–214.

Boden, M. A. (1972), *Purposive Explanation in Psychology* (Cambridge, Mass.: Harvard University Press).

Boden, M. A. (1977/87), *Artificial Intelligence and Natural Man* (NewYork: Basic Books, 1977). (2nd edn., expanded, 1987. London: MIT Press; NewYork: Basic Books.)

Boden, M. A. (1990/2004), *The Creative Mind: Myths and Mechanisms* (London: Weidenfeld & Nicolson, 1990). (2nd edn expanded/revised, London: Routledge, 2004.)

Boden, M. A. (1999), 'Is Metabolism Necessary?', *British Journal for the Philosophy of Science*, 50: 231–248.

Boden, M. A. (2006), *Mind as Machine: A History of Cognitive Science* (Oxford: The Clarendon Press).

Chomsky, A.N.(1995), *The Minimalist Program* (Cambridge, Mass.: MIT Press).

Chomsky, A.N., and Lasnik, H. (1977), 'Filters and Controls,' *Linguistic Inquiry*, 8: 425–504.

Chrisley, R.L. (2000), 'Transparent Computationalism', in M. Scheutz (ed.), *Computationalism – The Next Generation,* Proceedings of the Workshop New Trends in Cognitive Science 1999: (Vienna: Conceptus-Studien), 105–120.

Copley, P., and Gartland-Jones, A. (2005), 'Musical Form and Algorithmic Solutions', in L. Candy (ed.), *Creativity and Cognition 2005*: Proceedings of the Fifth Conference on Creativity and Cognition, 12–15 April, Goldsmiths College (NewYork: ACM Press), 226–231.

Dennett, D. C. (1988), 'Quining Qualia', in A. Marcel and E. Bisiach (eds.), *Consciousness in Contemporary Science* (Oxford: Oxford University Press), 42–77.

Dennett, D. C. (2005), *Sweet Dreams: Philosophical Obstacles to a Science of Consciousness* (Cambridge, Mass.: MIT Press).

Di Paolo, E. A. (1998), An Investigation into the Evolution of Communication', *Adaptive Behavior,* 6: 285–324.

Gazdar,G.J.M., Klein, E., Pullum, G., and Sag, I.A. (1985), *Generalized Phrase Structure Grammar* (Oxford: Blackwell).

Gross, P.R., and Levitt, N. (eds.), (1998), *Higher Superstition: The Academic Left and Its Quarrels with Science* (London: Johns Hopkins University Press). 2nd edn.

Hutchins, E.L. (1995), *Cognition in the Wild* (Cambridge, Mass.: MIT Press).

Marr, D.C. (1979), 'Representing and Computing Visual Information', in P.H.Winston and R.H. Brown (eds.), *Artificial Intelligence : An MIT Perspective, vol. 2* (Cambridge, Mass.: MIT Press), 17–82.

Masterman, M. (2007), *Language, Cohesion and Form,* ed. Y.A.Wilks. Cambridge: Cambridge University Press).

Miller, G.A., Galanter, E., and Pribram, K.H. (1960), *Plans and the Structure of Behavior* (New York: Holt).

Millikan, R.G. (1984), *Language, Thought, and Other Biological Categories: New Foundations for Realism* (Cambridge, Mass.: MIT Press).

Milner, A.D., and Goodale, M. A. (1993), 'Visual Pathways to Perception and Action', in T.P. Hicks, S. Molotchnikoff and T. Ono (eds.), *Progress in Brain Research*, vol. 95 (Amsterdam: Elsevier), 317–337.

Minsky, M.L.(1956/1961). 'Steps Toward Artificial Intelligence', Proceedings of the Institute of Radio Engineers, 49 (1961): 8–30. (First published in 1956 as an MIT Technical Report, *Heuristic Aspects of the Artificial Intelligence Problem.*)

Minsky, M.L. (1985), *The Society of Mind* (NewYork: Simon & Schuster).

Minsky, M.L. (2006), *The Emotion Machine: Commonsense Thinking, Artificial Intelligence and the Future of the Human Mind* (NewYork: Simon & Schuster).

Pollard, C., and Sag, I.A. (1994), *Head-driven Phrase Structure Grammar* (Chicago: University of Chicago Press).

Sampson, G.R., and McCarthy, D. (2004), *Corpus Linguistics: Readings in a Widening Discipline* (London: Continuum).

Scheutz, M. (ed.), *Computationalism: New Directions* (Cambridge, Mass.: MIT Press).

Sloman, A. (1978), *The Computer Revolution in Philosophy: Philosophy, Science, and Models of Mind* (Brighton: Harvester Press). Available, and continually updated, online at http://www.cs.bham.ac.uk/research/cogaff/crp/.

Sloman, A. (1983), 'Image Interpretation: The Way Ahead?', in O. J. Braddick and A. C. Sleigh (eds.), *Physical and Biological Processing of Images* (NewYork: Springer-Verlag), 380–402.

Sloman, A. (1986), 'What Sorts of Machine Can Understand the Symbols They Use?', *Proceedings of the Aristotelian Society, Supp.*, 60: 61–80.

Sloman, A. (1987), 'Reference Without Causal Links', in J.B.H. du Boulay., D. Hogg and L. Steels (eds.), *Advances in Artificial Intelligence – II* (Dordrecht: North Holland), 369–381.

Sloman, A. (1989), 'On Designing a Visual System: Towards a Gibsonian Computational Model of Vision', *Journal of Experimental and Theoretical AI*, 1: 289–337.

Sloman, A. (1995), 'Sim_agent helpfile', available at URL ftp://ftp.cs.bham.ac.uk/pub/dist/poplog/sim/help/sim_agent. See also 'Sim_agent web-page', available at URL http://www.cs.bham.ac.uk/axs/cog_affect/sim_agent.html.

Sloman, A. (1996a), 'Towards a General Theory of Representations', in D. M. Peterson (ed.), *Forms of Representation: An Interdisciplinary Theme for Cognitive Science* (Exeter: Intellect Books), 118–140.

Sloman, A. (1996b), 'Actual Possibilities', in L. C. Aiello and S. C. Shapiro (eds.), *Principles of Knowledge Representation and Reasoning: Proceedings of the Fifth International Conference* (KR '96) (San Francisco: Morgan Kaufmann), 627–638.

Sloman, A. (1999), 'Review of [R. Picard's] Affective Computing', *AI Magazine*, 20:1 (March), 127–133.

Sloman, A. (2002), 'The Irrelevance of Turing Machines to Artificial Intelligence', in M. Scheutz (ed.), *Computationalism: New Directions* (Cambridge, Mass.: MIT Press), 87–127.

Sloman, A., and Chrisley, R.L. (2003), 'Virtual Machines and Consciousness', in O. Holland (ed.), *Machine Consciousness* (Exeter: Imprint Academic), 133–172. Special issue of the *Journal of Consciousness Studies*, 10 (4–5). 133–172.

Sloman, A., and Poli, R. (1995), 'Sim_agent: A Toolkit for Exploring Agent Designs', in M. Wooldridge, J. Mueller and M. Tambe (eds.), *Intelligent Agents Vol. II* (Berlin: Springer-Verlag), 392–407.

Smith, B.C. (1985), 'Prologue to *Reflection and Semantics in a Procedural Language*', in R.J. Brachman and H. J. Levesque (eds.), *Readings in Knowledge Representation* (Los Altos, CA: Morgan Kauffman), 31–40.

Smith, B.C. (1996), *On the Origin of Objects* (Cambridge, Mass.: MIT Press).

Steels, L. (1998b), 'Synthesizing the Origins of Language and Meaning Using Co-Evolution, Self-Organization, and Level Formation', in J. R. Hurford, M. Studdert-Kennedy and C. Knight (eds.), *Approaches to the Evolution of Language: Social and Cognitive Bases* (Cambridge: Cambridge University Press), 384–405.

Strauss, C., and Quinn, N. (1997), *A Cognitive Theory of Cultural Meaning*, Series: Publications of the Society for Psychological Anthropology (Cambridge: Cambridge University Press).

Thornton, C. J. (2005), '*A Quantitative Reconstruction of Boden's Creativity Theory*', (University of Sussex: Dept. of Informatics).

Wiggins, G. A. (2001), 'Towards a More Precise Characterisation of Creativity', in R. Weber and C.G. von Wangenheim (eds.), *Case-Based Reasoning* (Washington DC: Navy Center for Applied Research in Artificial Intelligence), 113–120.

Wright, I. P., and Sloman, A. (1997), *MINDER1: An Implementation of a Protoemotional Agent Architecture*. Technical Report CSRP-97-1, University of Birmingham, School of Computer Science.(Available from ftp://ftp.cs.bham.ac.uk/pub/tech-reports/1997/CSRP-97-01.ps.gz)

Wright, I.P., Sloman, A., and Beaudoin, L. P. (1996), 'Towards a Design-Based Analysis of Emotional Episodes', *Philosophy, Psychiatry, and Psychology*, 3: 101–137.

2

Valentino Braitenberg

Director Emeritus

Max Planck Institute for Biological Cybernetics

and Institute of Medical Psychology, University of Tuebingen

Germany

---

1. Why were you initially drawn to computational and/or informational issues?

When I was about 10 years old, in the mid-thirties of the last century, I tried hard to invent a non-vacuum amplifying device, something like a transistor, since I was too poor to buy commercial vacuum tubes and (justifiably) did not feel up to making one myself. I tried pieces of wood with wires attached in various positions, also pieces of charcoal and of various rocks and crystals. Nothing seemed to work, or perhaps my naive measuring devices were insufficient. I also had a drawer in my desk full of an incredible mess of wires. I dreamt of putting my quasi-transistors (the word, let alone the thinghad not yet been invented at the time) in the places where the wires touched each otherand felt that thereby the whole thing would turn into – what?A thinking machine? A computer? A living being? The smell of these future developments was just around the corner, distinctly perceptible to many millions of little boys like me. So please don't ask what it was that drew us to computational and informational issues.

2. What example(s) from your work (or the work of others) best illustrates the fruitful use of a computational and/or informational approach for foundational researches and/or applications?

It is now almost exactly half a century since I started to look through the microscope in my lab at real neural networks in various animal brains. Thiswas not a fashionable endeavour in 1948.At that time, the fat tomes by Golgi and Ramon y Cajal were collecting dust in the libraries, while the neuronaldiagrams they contained were shown around as evidence of a ludicrous, old-fashioned, rococo,playfulness far removed from the then modern issues of EEG and fibre tract anatomy.What I saw in those drawings, and then in my own histological preparations, was something else: circuit diagrams, memories of my childish phase of radio engineering, networks of a complexity far beyond what electronic engineers even deemed possible. It was complexity that struck us, not only in the brain, but generally in living matter everywhere, and in the products of the human spirit such as language and thought. And what filled us with happiness and enthusiasm, was a bit of theory that promised to tie the science of complexity with its associated psychological meanings to the bulk of hard science through a neat statistical interpretation. We read Shannon's Information Theory and had the impression that from now on we were not to worry any more about the chasm separating mind and physics. And we read Wiener's Cybernetics and gained the feeling that we were in very good company in this brave new world.

In answer to the second question: at least three of my pet projects would have been unthinkable if not for the background of this revolution of computation and information: the interpretation of the cerebellum as a time-measuring device, the analysis of a neural network in the fly's eye where every single fibre was given an unmistakable computational role, and the structure of the cerebral cortex as a probabilistic computer.

3. What is the proper role of computer science and/or information theory in relation to other disciplines, including other philosophical areas?

The concept of information, properly understood, is fully sufficient to do away with popular dualistic schemes invoking spiritual substances distinct from anything in physics. This is Aristotle *redivivus*, the concept of matter and form united in every object of this world, body and soul, where the latter is nothing but the formal aspect of the former. The very term "information" clearly demonstrates its Aristotelian origin in its linguistic root.

Students of the anatomy and physiology of the brain may take comfort in this. They are not only studying the matrix in which things spiritual develop and move, but rather are putting their hands on the soul itself as the ensemble of rules and constraints which defines the brain.

4. What do you consider the most neglected topics and/or contributions in late 20th century studies of computation and/or information?

I believe we should have pursued the study of language with greater energy, both at the level of cerebral mechanisms responsible for the production and understanding of language and at the more abstract level of the structure of language itself. Quite apart from the impelling necessity of mechanizing linguistic communication in an increasingly multiethnic world, language offers a window on brain function where it is most interesting, in its sequential aspects.

5. What are the most important open problems concerning computation and/or information and what are the prospects for progress?

Quite generally, the main problem can be formulated thus. Memory is acquisition of knowledge by the brain, i.e. incorporation of the redundancies which are present in the sensory inflow from the environment, either in the course of evolution or by individual learning. This implies the study of these redundancies as well as of the way they are represented in the brain. The first problem is simply that of physics, the second belongs to brain physiology. The two sciences may be well advised to coordinate their efforts.

3

Brian Cantwell-Smith

Dean of the Faculty of Information Studies
University of Toronto, Canada

From E&M to M&E[1]
A journey through the landscape of computing

Not only are the philosophy of computing and the philosophy of information new fields, still theoretically unstable, but the subject matters they span are exceptionally broad. "Information" covers so many phenomena as to be threatened by vacuity – though that hasn't deterred people from using it as an explanatory concept in fields as diverse as biology , computer science, medicine, journalism, electrical engineering, literature, the arts. Computation is narrower, and seems better understood, in part because of half a century's work on mathematical theories of computability. But here I believe appearances are misleading. Not only do we not understand computing as well as is generally thought, I will argue, but making progress will require upending all sorts of fundamental assumptions in ontology, epistemology, and even metaphysics.

This combination of newness and breadth means that no contributor to this volume can assure the reader that the path they have traveled through the landscape may not be due as much to their own philosophical predilections as to any intrinsic geography. So there is merit to Floridi's suggestion that we start with biographic details. However it also means that all writing in these areas (my own included) is liable to fall prey to Isaiah Berlin's challenge that "writing is amateur when you learn about the author, not about the subject matter."

---

[1] "E&M" is physics' moniker for "electricity and magnetism," the field from which I entered computing. "M&E" is philosophy's parallel epithet for "metaphysics and epistemology," the landscape to which my travels through computation have led.

Forewarned is forearmed.

1. Origins

My own interest stems from my first semester at university, when
an IBM 360/44 was delivered into the basement of the Oberlin College physics department. Driven by a naïve version of C.P. Snow's
two-culture dilemma, I wrestled with whether to drop physics and
major in religion, debated politics with anyone who was awake,
and spent the remainder of my nights ferrying stuffed boxes of
punched cards back and forth to the operator's window at the
Computing Center. Crazed, yes; but it made a kind of manic sense.
Knowing nothing of hermetic methods or intellectual precursors,
I was possessed by a conviction that the power and elegance of
science, the gravity and richness of politics and religion, and the
intensity of intimate human communion were ultimately more similar than they were different.

Within two months I had made two life-altering decisions. First,
I vowed to dig deep enough to get to the place where these superficially different perspectives could be understood, if not as "one,"
then at least as *integral* – as part of a single encompassing reality.
Second, at a more pedestrian level, I asked my physics professor
for 6 weeks off from doing problem sets, to figure out whether the
school's new computer might help with this quest. What I wanted
to know, I told him, was whether computing could be understood
with all the power and insight and elegance that I loved in the
sciences, but nevertheless do justice, in a way no prior scientific
account ever had, to the richness and complexity of the human
condition.

It was a classic sophomoric venture: wisdom shot through with
foolishness. All told, it wasn't a bad question. But six weeks turned
into forty years.

The first results stemmed from those long nights of debugging.
Inchoately at first, but more articulately as the years went by, I
came to believe that the understanding of computing I was deriving from concrete engagement – not just at Oberlin, but later writing operating systems, implementing data bases, designing programming languages – was not accounted for by what was being
taught about computing in the nascent field of computer science.
The problem wasn't just that theories idealized, or ignored the
practical realities one had to come to grips with in real-world settings. As much is true of any engineering practice. Rather, I could

never shake the feeling that the accounts were profoundly wrong, misguided at their core – "missing" what mattered most about the territory we were tacitly and somewhat blindly exploring.

In parallel, motivated by an interest in people and mind, I was drawn into artificial intelligence (AI) and cognitive science, initiatives whose fortunes were on the rise, as society grappled with the monumental idea that computing was not just a technology of disruptive impact, but also a powerful *idea* – perhaps even one that applied to us. *Maybe we, too, were computers.* Debates raged, with endorsements rung from the MIT, Carnegie Mellon, and Stanford AI laboratories,[2] critiques lobbed back by Weizenbaum, Dreyfus, and Searle,[3] and more speculative analyses taken up across the philosophy of mind.[4]

Naturally, I wanted to formulate my own position. But I was blocked by my underlying sense of discrepancy between *how we thought computers worked* and my blood-and-bones intuitions as to *how they actually worked.* The situation is depicted in figure 1. Debate on what came to be known as *the computational theory of mind* (CTOM) was presumed to have the structure labeled α. What it is to be a *computer* was assumed to be uncontentiously formulated in the "received" theory of computation, labeled θ_c in the diagram. At stake was how to understand the *mind:* θ_m. The substance of the CTOM was taken to be the thesis that $\theta_m \approx \theta_c$.[5]

---

[2] Particularly Marvin Minsky & Seymour Papert at MIT, Allen Newell and Herbert Simon at Carnegie Mellon (CMU), and John McCarthy at Stanford.

[3] Especially Joseph Weizenbaum's ELIZA program [1966], Hubert Dreyfus' *What Computers Can't Do: A Critique of Artificial Intelligence* [1972], and John Searle's "Chinese Room" thought experiment [1980].

[4] E.g., Haugeland's *Mind Design* [1981], and *Artificial Intelligence: The Very Idea* [1985]. Mid 19th-century philosophical discussions of computing were primarily conducted in the philosophy of mathematics, pursuant to Gödel's proof and Turing's computability results; by the end of the century, the debate had moved to the philosophy of mind. It is only now that an authentic philosophy of computing is coming into its own.

[5] Not, of course, that anyone thought that *all* computers were minds (M = C). Even if all minds are computational, the class of computers is larger, and so clearly M ⊂ C. This raises the question of how what was *specific* to mind, and how that would be articulated. The complexity of the questions was rarely explicitly addressed, but it was presumed that the restriction of C to M would also be expressed *in computational terms*—as opposed, say, to minds being those computers that "weigh more than 1 lb but less than 10," a restriction that leaves minds as computers, but where the restriction itself is not, as it were, a "computational" restriction, not being framed in terms of a property (weight) that is itself a "computational property."

My problem was straightforward. Fundamentally, I took the CTOM not to be a theory-laden proposition, in the sense of framing or resting on a specific hypothesis θ_c about what computers are, independent of whether θ_c held of real-world computers. Rather, I took it to have an ostensive or "transparent" character (β): that people (i.e., us) are computers *in whatever way that computers (i.e., those things over there) are computers* – or at least in whatever way *some* of those things are or might be computers.[6] It wouldn't be interesting, I felt (this was no attempt to vindicate Weizenbaum, Dreyfus or Searle), if it emerged that, sure enough, θ_c wasn't true of people, but θ_c *wasn't true of the ibm* 360, *abs brake systems, or my word processor, either.* Suppose, in particular, as I suspected, that θ_c was not the right theory of computing, but instead that $\theta_{c'}$, or $\theta_{c''}$, or some other account, were "correct" or anyway to be preferred?[7] Then the only interesting question, I believed, was whether $\theta_{c'}$ or $\theta_{c''}$ (or whatever) held of people.

A myriad challenges can be raised against this approach, including: that an "empirical" stance cannot be right, because θ_c (i.e., the accepted mathematical theory of computation and computability) is *how computing is defined*; that because we build computers, we *must* understand them; etc. While I disagree with all of this, this is not the place to address it. The point is simply that I believed (i) that the only interesting version of the CTOM needed a theory that did justice to computing, and (ii) that θ_c was not it. And so, around the mid 1970s, I took up the project that occupied me for the next 25 years: to *figure out what computing is* (i.e., which variant of θ_c is right), at a level of depth strong enough to found an adequate theory of computing, and richly enough articulated to support substantive debate about a relevant computational theory of mind.

Before I could address the question of whether the CTOM was true, that is, I needed to know what it said.

By 1972 I had moved to MIT, an epicenter of AI and cognitive science. Instead of entering those programs directly, I first enrolled as a "social inquiry" major – reflecting my interest in assessing, rather than embracing, the CTOM. But the same problem of inadequacy in reigning conceptions of computing impeded my participation in that fledgling STS program – for example, the

---

[6] Cf. footnote 4.

[7] Whatever "correct" comes to, whether that is even the right term, etc. For simplicity, I have phrased the issue conservatively.

assumption that computing is a *technology*, as opposed, say, to a form of art or sculpture. Recognizing that insight could only come from substantial engagement, I transferred to the Artificial Intelligence Laboratory for the remainder of my education.

2. Preliminaries

Philosophy of computing is in its infancy. Whether history will even notice us I do not know, but we have certainly just scratched its surface. Take a dozen terms of the computational art: *program, process, algorithm, symbol, data structure, implementation, architecture, complexity, object-oriented, user-friendly, nondeterminism,* and *procedural.* Every one remains unreconstructed – some more so than others, but all to an extent that five minutes in an undergraduate class is enough to raise questions that outstrip contemporary comprehension. Even such fundamental notions as *being computational, carrying information, being algorithmic or effective,* etc., remain open – no one knows whether they are: *intrinsic,* like mass and momentum; *abstract,* like numbers or types; *relational,* like being well-loved; or require *external ascription* or *interpretation,* like the meanings of books and text.[8]

I do not say this to be negative. On the contrary, the inchoate state of our understanding greatly energizes the field. It is like participating in the early days of physics. Graduate students can still read everything that has been written, and set out to explore largely uncharted intellectual realms. Critical issues are at stake – not just fundamental ones of meaning, mechanism, and reality – but also such notions as credibility, authenticity, engagement, and the like.

Nevertheless, the modest state of the art does suggest that students enter the field with some humility, lest they be misled into taking more for granted than is warranted. Four cautions strike me as especially important:

C1 *Computers, computing, computation:* It is essential not to assume pretheoretically any particular conception of – or distinction among – such familiar notions as *computer, computing, computation, computable,* etc. One such view has become something of a commonplace in computer science: that *computations,* viewed

---

[8]Everyone, including myself, can raise objections to every one of these examples, and to the four-way typology. That is the point. The intellectual structure of the inquiry is still up for grabs.

as abstract objects, are the entities of theoretical interest; and that *computers*, merely physical devices that realize or implement computations, are of no theoretical significance (no matter how economically and pragmatically consequential). This is the stance immortalized in Dijkstra's famous claim that "computer science is no more about computers than astronomy is about telescopes." But any substance to that blunt pronouncement,[9] including the distinctions it is framed in terms of, depend on a theoretical framework the adequacy of which should be in question in any foundational analysis.[10]

C2 *Equivalence:* It is critical not to give undue weight, especially conceptual weight, to the famous equivalence proofs underlying mathematical computability – proofs according to which various different "models" of computing (Turing machines, the λ-calculus, Kleene's recursion equations, etc.[11]) are shown to "compute" the same class of mathematical functions. Not only is the legitimacy of these proofs rarely questioned; it is also common to assume—falsely, in my view—that they show that the different models are "equivalent" for other purposes as well. Some illustrative problems:

a. As in C1, the proofs rely on a conception of what it is to "compute" – a notion that should be questioned, not assumed, in a foundational account. To assume such "post-theoretic" equivalences in advance will inevitably prejudice, and at worst render circular, any account of computing based on them.

b. The notion of "compute" on which the equivalence proofs rely is extremely restricted. Issues of input and output, and any other form of interaction or engagement with the world, are not so much ignored as banished – kept outside the framework. No mention is made of how the tape is initialized, how the results are "read out" (or interpreted; see C4), or anything of the sort. Time and timing are similarly dismissed. While complexity analyses pay some attention to resources, the claim that a universal machine can do "anything" – at least, "anything that can be done by machine" – is excruciatingly narrow. Tap out the differences among rhumba, reggae, and bebop? Make a cup of coffee? "Out of bounds!" is the

---

[9] With which, as it happens but perhaps not surprisingly, I disagree.

[10] Note the contrast with cognitive science and philosophy of mind, which (especially in the analytic tradition) used to view "mind" as essentially independent of body - a dualism that has come crashing down in recent years.

[11] Paradigmatically, devices of minimal structure given access to indefinite storage.

standard reply. But who said so – and why? These are things a
philosophical analysis should explain, not presume.

c. Conversely, the equivalence metric used in the equivalence
proofs is extraordinarily broad – so broad as to sweep under the
rug virtually every distinction that might be relevant to a theory of
mind: how the device works; whether the resulting computation is
intrinsic, ascribed, relative, relational, etc.; how long it would take
to run; and so on. The standard way one shows that one machine
can "do the same thing" as another, in fact, is to have the first
machine *model* or *simulate* the second – the very distinction on
which Searle based his critical distinction between "weak" and
"strong" AI.[12] Distinctions on which competing theories of mind
are distinguished – behaviourism , representationalism, type or
token reductionism, materialism, etc. – are similarly obliterated
in the quest for isomorphism.

d. All semantic issues, about meaning and interpretation, are
again ignored or banned. In his original work on information theory Shannon was particularly articulate about this setting aside
of issues of meaning and content; for reasons described below, the
situation in computing is more complex. But independent of the
use of *words*, fundamental issues of how systems signify, represent,
carry information about, are interpreted as, or otherwise relate to
the world around them are not addressed by any received theory
of computing.

C3 *Semantic Soup:* In days of Ptolemaic and pre-Copernican
astronomy, it was easy to distinguish among the various accou-
trements of inquiry: *theory, experiment, equipment, model, representation, subject matter,* etc. Theories were viewed as abstract;
representations were written down, probably on parchment; models, such as brass orreries, likely sat on tables; celestial subject
matters were a long way away. In computational times, however,
one encounters claims that instances of all these categories are
of the same kind: computational processes of one sort or other.[13]
Even in Turing's original paper, distinctions among numbers, representations of numbers, and numeric models are conflated after
just a few pages. The mathematical proofs mentioned above, along
with such kin as Gödel's incompleteness theorems, category the-

---

[12] Just because x simulates y, that doesn't mean that x *is* y. Searle J.
(1980) "Minds, Brains and Programs" *Behavioral and Brain Sciences* **3** (3):
417-457,

[13] I am not saying a theory *can* be a computation (as opposed to something
more abstract); merely, that some people claim so.

ory, and the like, identify (i.e., conflate) all manner of isomorphic things. Current writers sometimes muse about the overlap,[14] but by and large it receives little attention. The caution, here, is not so much an injunction *not to do* this or that, but to keep a strict eye on the soup of semantic relationships in which computational systems simmer, lest the intentional character of the phenomenon dissolve from view.

C4 *Mathematics:* In part because of the prior three cautions, I enjoin students never to use mathematical examples as paradigmatic illustrations of computing, or as case studies on top of which to develop a general account. Numbers, numerals, mathematical models, and the like are simply too easy to confuse or conflate for it to be possible to "extract" the true nature of what is going on. Not only that; people's philosophies of mathematics differ by more than the issues at stake in philosophy of computing and/or philosophy of mind. Some people take numbers to be concepts; others, to be Platonic abstractions; still others, to be numerals or expressions; etc. How can one forge a cogent philosophy of computing in the face of such ontological profusion? Better to pervert Gertrude Stein to our purposes: "Forget numbers; think about potatoes."

By way of preparation, especially for those new to the field, two additional observations need to be added to these four cautions:[15]

P1 *Terminological Archeology:* Much of the theoretical vocabulary we use to study computing was not invented *de novo*. A great many terms of art were borrowed from logic and metamathematics – the areas in which Turing, Kleene, and other computational progenitors worked. Thus such notions as *syntax, semantics, symbol, identifier, variable, reference, interpretation, model,* etc., were used technically in logic long before they were pressed into computational service. This overlap has generated more confusion, I believe, than has been adequately recognized.

Searle's two arguments against the possibility of artificial intelligence are striking examples: (i) his "Chinese Room" argument, that semantics does not inhere in syntax; and (ii) his parallel argument that syntax does not inhere in physics.[16] Searle was trained as a philosopher, and would have learned the words 'syntax,' 'se-

---

[14] Cf. Edelman's ironic comment that he had validated his emphatically *non-computational* model by "implementing it on a computer." Edelman G.M. 2007, *Second Nature: Brain Science and Human Knowledge*

[15] It will be obvious later why these two deserve mention here.

[16] Chapter 9 of *Rediscovering the Mind*, MIT Press, 1992.

mantics,' 'formal,' etc., from logic. As far as I know, computer scientists, on reading his arguments, feel that Searle "just doesn't get it." What I have told students for more than 20 years, however, is that *Searle would have been right, if the words meant what he was taught that they mean* – if, that is, by 'syntax' and 'semantics,' computer scientists meant what the people they took those words from (i.e., logicians) meant by those terms. This is not to excuse Searle, whose conclusions I am not endorsing;[17] but it does throw down a gauntlet that we say, *in language that non-computer scientists can understand*, what computing is. Yet another reason why the philosophy of computing is so important.

P2 *Interdisciplinary Theory:* Finally, it pays to attend to the relations between substantive issues that arise in computing and allied questions addressed in other fields – especially as the place of computing in the overall intellectual landscape is not yet well understood or agreed. Just one example: computer science has extensive vocabulary to talk about the relation between one system understood as "an α" and that very same system understood as "a β" – i.e., as we say, *one and the same system analysed at different levels of abstraction.* As well as using such basic terms as 'implementation' and 'realization,' computational discussions involve such notions as *abstraction, modularity, "black-box" and "grey-box" implementation boundaries, importation, exportation, interoperability protocols, interfaces* (including APIs), etc. Philosophy of mind and philosophy of science have developed their own theoretical apparatus to deal with what looks at first blush to be the same subject – under such terms as *type-* and *token-reduction,* (local and global) *supervenience, multiple realisability,* etc.

For years I have offered to supervise a doctoral student to conduct a theoretical analysis of trans-disciplinary vocabulary in this or various allied areas, since I am not aware of any other systematic investigation of how the two analytic frameworks relate. No takers so far, but the offer remains open.

Enough preliminaries. Once the land is cleared, the project of developing an adequate philosophy of computing opens up into something like Frege's investigation of number – except that the empirical commitment requires maintaining focus on concrete, in-

---

[17]I agree with him, as it happens, both that syntax does not inhere in physics, and that semantics does not inhere in syntax - at least on local interpretations of all those words. Where I disagree with him is on the underlying assumption that computation is syntactic.

the-world phenomena. In that way it is also reminiscent of questions in the foundations of physics: about meaning, interpretation, measurement, and reality.

It does rather mean starting from scratch. But such is the nature of the enterprise.

3. Project

Given these considerations, how can one proceed? My approach has been to intersect three cross-cutting "axes" along which computation has historically been analysed – generating something like an informal coordinate system in terms of which to map the computational territory. In no way do I endorse the resulting cartography as theoretically sound, or even as particularly coherent. By the time I am done, in fact, I discard every one of these distinctions, or reconfigure them beyond recognition. Still, the system pays its way as an initial guide.

3a Construals

The first axis enumerates seven "construals" of computing, as I put it, that have variously held sway in our intellectual discourse:

- *Formal Symbol Manipulation* (FSM): the idea, derivative from a century's work in formal logic and metamathematics, of a machine manipulating symbolic or (at least potentially) meaningful expressions independent of their interpretation or semantic content;

- *Effective Computability* (EC): what can be done, and how hard it is to do it, "mechanically," as it were, by (an abstract analogue of?) a "mere machine";

- *Execution of an Algorithm* (ALG) or *Rule-Following* (RF): what is involved, and what behaviour is thereby produced, in following a set of rules or instructions, such as when making dessert;

- *Calculation of a Function* (FUN): the behaviour, when given as input an argument to a mathematical function, of producing as output the value of that function applied to that argument;

- *Digital State Machine* (DSM): the idea of an automaton with a finite, disjoint set of internally homogeneous machine states – as parodied in the "clunk, clunk, clunk" gait of a 1950's cartoon robot;

- *Information Processing* (IP): what is involved in storing, manipulating, displaying, and otherwise trafficking in information, whatever information might be;

- *Physical Symbol Systems* (PSS): the idea, made famous by Newell and Simon (1976), that, somehow or other, computers interact with, and perhaps also are made of, symbols in a way that depends on their mutual physical embodiment.

I don't claim this list is exhaustive. Several more have recently made it onto the scene: non-linear dynamics, complex adaptive systems, a view of computing in terms of interacting agents, and so forth – all of which could be used to extend the list. Contrapuntally, a host of familiar ideas must be set aside as inappropriate for foundational duty: (i) demeaning characterisations, that computing is *just* something or other (machine, mechanism, artefact, attributed, etc.); (ii) negative construals, such as that computing is *not* some way (conscious, original, alive, and so on); and (iii) "higher-order" or adverbial specifications, such as *abstract, universal, formal,* etc., which only gain traction against some presumed prior property. The members of all three categories implicitly rely on another conception of computing, in order to have any substance.[18] But leaving such complexifications aside, it is the seven listed above – what I call the classic construals – that, at least to date, have shouldered the weight of the intellectual debate.

It is critical to recognise that all seven construals are both intensionally (conceptually) and extensionally distinct. In part because of their great familiarity, and in part because "real" computers apparently exemplify more than one of them, but perhaps especially because of the pernicious influence of those pesky equivalence proofs, it is often thought that the seven are roughly synonymous. This conflationary tendency has been especially rampant in cognitive science and philosophy of mind, both of which tend to move around among the seven with abandon. But to do so is a mistake. The supposition that any two of these construals amount to the same thing, let alone the whole group, is simply false.[19]

---

[18] How do we know that computers are just machines, not conscious, etc.? Only if we have some other account of what they are like, from which such a conclusion could then be derived.

[19] Formal symbol manipulation is explicitly characterized in terms of a se-

Clarifying the issues raised in these construals, bringing salient assumptions to the fore, showing where they agree and where they differ, tracing the roles they have played in computing's first century – questions like this must be part of any foundational reconstruction. But in a sense these issues are all secondary. For none has the bite of the reason we are interested in the set in the first place: whether any of the enumerated accounts is *right*.

That question, too, must be addressed: to what jury a pro-

---

mantic aspect of computation, for example, if for no other reason than that without it there would be no warrant in calling it *symbol* manipulation—to say nothing of there being nothing for it to work independently of. The digital state machine construal, in contrast, makes no such reference to semantic properties. If a Lincoln-log contraption were digital but not symbolic, and a continuous symbol machine were formal but not digital, they would be differentially counted as computational by the two construals. Not only do FSM and DSM *mean* different things, in other words; they have overlapping but distinct extensions.

The effective computability and algorithm execution construals also differ on semantics. Whereas effective computability seems free of intentional connotation, the idea of algorithm execution seems not only to involve rules or recipes, which presumably do mean something, but also to require something like "understanding" or at least "semantic compliance" on the part of the agent producing the behavior. It is also unclear whether the notions of "machine" and "effectiveness" refer to causal powers, material realization, or other physical properties—or, as current theoretical discussions suggest, effective computability should be taken as an abstract mathematical notion. (This is no small question; if we do not yet understand the *mind/body problem for machines,* how can we expect computational metaphors to help us in the case of people?) The construals also differ on whether they focus on internal structure or on input/output—i.e., on whether (i) they treat computation as *a way of being structured or constituted*, so that surface behavior is derivative (FSM and DSM), or whether the *having of a particular surface behavior* is the essential locus of computationality, with questions about how that is achieved left unspecified and uncared about (EC, perhaps ALG).

Not only must the construals be distinguished, moreover; further distinctions are required within each one. Thus the notion of information processing—responsible for such slogans as *The Information Age*, and the link between philosophy of computing and philosophy of information—must be broken down into at least three sub-readings,depending on how *information* is understood: (i) as a lay notion, dating from perhaps the 19th century, of an abstract, publicly-accessible commodity carrying a degree of autonomous authority; (ii) so-called "information theory," the semantics-free notion originating with Shannon & Weaver (1949), which spread out through much of cybernetics and communication theory, is implicated in Kolmogorov and other complexity measures, and has been tied to notions of energy and entropy; and (iii) the semantical notion of information advocated by Dretske (1981), Barwise & Perry (1983), Halpern (1987), and others.

posed theory of computing should be held accountable. But for now let me cut straight to the chase: *not one is correct.* Forty years after that freshman year in college, I am prepared to argue that, when subjected to the empirical demands of practice and the conceptual demands of theory, *all seven construals fail* – for deep, overlapping, but distinct, reasons. No one of them, nor any group in combination, is adequate to meet the requirements of a foundational account.

3b Dialectics

To understand the reason for this failure, and grasp the picture of computing that comes out of it, it helps to identify the other two "axes" I use as an initial guide to the territory – both of which cross-cut the first division into construals.

The second involves a set of 4 "dialectics" – fundamental metaphysical distinctions particularly applicable to "things computational," and necessary to understand if we are to claim to have an intellectual grasp on computing.

1 *Meaning and mechanism:* The first dialectic involves the only substantial thesis about the nature of computing I adopt as an investigative guide (again, not as necessarily true of the subject matter, but indicative of issues to be investigated): that, in one way or other, computation involves an interaction or interplay of *meaning* and *mechanism.* That computation is somehow mechanical is reflected in the fundamental effectiveness limits that permeate computational theory and experience. As already suggested, there is disagreement about the nature or origin of this "efficacy" – whether it is (i) an abstract notion, as gestured towards in the notion of an "effectively computable function," taken by logicians and mathematicians to be an entirely abstract notion, unrelated to physical constraint; or (ii) a physical notion, tied to underlying physical law. But as so powerfully demonstrated by Turing in his original paper, that computation is in one way or another limited both in principle and in practice is as deep a fact about the topic as any that exists.[20]

That computation has anything to do with meaning, interpretation, semantics, etc., is much less widely agreed – in spite of the use of logical language discussed above. I take the semantic nature of computing to be compelling, however, both from the na-

---

[20] Students think Turing is famous because he introduced the notion of a computer, and demonstrated its power. It is important to remind them that he demonstrated *both its power and its limitation.*

ture of existing theoretical debate and from the character of the phenomenon.

2 *Abstract and concrete:* A second distinction that permeates computing, which has arisen several times already, is that between the *concrete* and the *abstract*. What "degree of concreteness" computation manifests, if I can put the question that way, is deucedly difficult to figure out – to say nothing of what, under scrutiny, the terms even mean. Are arrangements of physical things themselves physical, abstract, or somewhere in between? ("I like what you've done with your living room; that's a *great arrangement of chairs*.") What about abstractly specified concrete properties, or concretely specified abstract properties? Or do the words signify neither a binary distinction, nor two ends of a continuum, but some third possibility entirely? Perhaps they aren't even the right contrast pair. Only the philosophy of computing knows for sure.

3 *Static and dynamic:* Less philosophically vexed, but as crucial to computing, is the distinction between *static* and *dynamic*. Programs, it would seem, are static entities, or anyway passive;[21] compilers translate them into other static entities (programs in a lower-level language); interpreters "run them," generating dynamic processes, etc. Or rather: interpreters are programs too; it is when interpreters *run* that they take programs and generate further process or behaviour – behaviour somehow different from, and yet in other ways coincident with, the behaviour of the interpreter's own running.

Some immediate facts aren't hard to delineate, in other words – even if the saying gets pedantic. Still, the distinction is important, as is the question of whether the way we currently arrange things is necessary or mere historical contingency. Is it just habit, or lack of imagination, that makes us think process specification should take static form? Could a dynamic process itself describe, represent, or specify?[22] If so, surely there could be computational analogues, suggesting that we shouldn't build static specification into our framework. In this and other cases, it is clearly important, in so far as it is possible, to avoid shackling our philosophy of computing to the tiny fraction of possible computational architectures that have so far been explored.

---

[21] This is not to say that people don't update them - i.e., make better versions *of the same program*; the identity conditions are complex, but programs certainly exist over time.

[22] Ask a friend to describe a spiral staircase, and watch their hands; you will see a dynamic representation.

4 *One and many:* Finally, any account of computing worth its salt must deal with a bewildering plethora of distinctions between "things that are one" and "things that are many," such as a single program, web page, file, etc., and multiple distributed "copies" or "versions" of it (a distinction that bedevils software projects and replicated data bases), or the issues that arise when you call a procedure on a matrix: do you pass a distinct copy or, as it is said, "the address," so that there is only one – or is that rather a new copy of "the same address," i.e., two pointers (copies?) that point to the same location, or ... . Attempts at ultimate clarity can lead to madness.[23]

We speak of many/one relations in many different ways: (i) in terms of *types, classes, categories, templates, patterns, schemata,* etc., where a single (abstract?) entity is taken to have multiple *instances;* (ii) as a (concrete?) unit thing with different *copies, editions,* or *versions;* (iii) as a *set* with distinct *members;* (iv) as a *role* played by different *individuals;* and so on. It is far from clear that we understand the distinctions between and among these ways of speaking, and why, exactly, we use one or other in any given case. More seriously, the profusion of possibilities, and the diabolical fact that on reflection whether something is "one" or "many" can seem to be a matter of perspective or even degree, rather than being an intrinsic property (of it? them?), can send metaphysical tremors through the foundations.

Another issue on which to keep an eagle eye.

3c Formality

The third axis has to do with formality – one of the most recalcitrant properties underlying the entire field. Somehow or other, it is thought, computation is a *formal* phenomenon, or amenable to *formal* analysis, or works *formally,* or something like that. Just which of these is true, what they mean, and how they relate, are additional issues that any philosophical analysis of computing must investigate.

The near-universal allegiance to formality is both curious and fertile. It is not as if "formal" is a technical or theory-internal predicate, after all–no one writes FORMAL(x) in their equations. Moreover, informal usage seems to range across as many as a dozen meanings of the term: *precise, abstract, syntactic, mathematical,*

---

[23] It is uncanny how sophisticated expert programmers are at navigating these singular/plural shoals.

explicit, digital, a-contextual, non-semantic, etc. Far from engendering debate, this profusion or outright ambiguity has probably helped to cement consensus. Because it remains tacit, cuts deep, has important historical roots, and permeates practice, formality is an ideal foil with which to investigate computation.

Once again I will cut straight to the bottom line. The moral for computer and cognitive science here is similar to the claim made earlier about the seven construals: *no plausible reading of 'formal,'* in my view, *applies to the computational case.* Needless to say, negative claims are tricky to prove. To make such a conclusion watertight, one would need both an agreed theory of computing and a definitive analysis of 'formality.' But certainly my investigations have led me to conclude that there is no substantive reading of 'formal' under which concrete, in-the-world computing – *computation in the wild,* as I sometimes call it – is, in fact, necessarily formal. As I put it in another context, "one cannot avoid the ultimately ironic conclusion: that the computer, darling child of the formal tradition, outstrips the bounds of the very tradition that gave rise to it."

4 Results

The issues discussed above are given slightly more treatment in Smith (1996), and will be explored in depth in Smith (forthcoming). Here, though, it is time to assemble these piecemeal results into the ultimate conclusion, and sketch some of the issues it opens up in front of us.

The bottom line again is simple. Not only do none of the seven construals, understood formally or informally, serve as an adequate account of computing. More seriously, no other construal, of my own or anyone else's making, will serve either. The reason is stark: *there is no theory of computing to be had.* This, too, is a result that after this long journey I am prepared to claim: the term 'computational' does not name a property of theoretical significance.[24] A philosopher who believed in such things might say that *computation is not a natural kind,* though not being such a philosopher, that is not how I would put it. I would rather just say this: that there is ultimately nothing *special* about computing or computers – nothing to give substance to a theoretical notion of computing – beyond the thesis of the first dialectic: computers

---

[24] Or *computing,* or *computer;* it doesn't matter.

are systems or devices that involve an interplay of meaning and mechanism, the best we know how to build. Period.

There is nothing more to say.

The first comment to make – and it should be made straight away – is that this is a wildly optimistic claim. Far from being negative, the fact that there is no theoretical substance to something's being computational (i) not only opens up the realm of computing to possibilities not heretofore imagined, but (ii) from an intellectual point of view, makes the development of computers vastly more significant than it would otherwise have been. Sure enough, a number of popular hypotheses end up on the cutting room floor – including the vaunted computational theory of mind.[25] On the other hand, it follows that all of the specific details and understandings and intricacies and mechanisms and architectures developed in computer science are "unrestricted": rather than applying to just a *subset* of the world's systems, they apply to *all* systems – at least all that involve the fundamental meaning/mechanism dialectic, which is a lot. So to take just one example: the relation discussed above between philosophy's notions of reduction, supervenience, etc., and computer science's understanding of architecture, implementation, abstraction boundaries, etc., are not just *parallel* developments. First blush was right: they are theoretical perspectives on *the same subject matter*. That is why that doctoral dissertation would be important – a synthesis of the two perspectives is mandated by the simple but compelling fact that the subject matters do in fact coincide.

I am not saying that the development of computing is not a theoretical (as well as practical) accomplishment of the utmost magnitude. The discovery of how to arrange physical matter in such a way as to implement digital processes, for example, is a staggering achievement – easily worth a passel of Nobel prizes. Rather, the point is that, instead of being viewed as a restricted species, as is implicit in the idea that 'computational' is a property of theoretical significance, computers are better understood as a *site* – a "laboratory of middling complexity," where we can work out the best understandings we can muster about how meaning and mechanism interact.

---

[25] Of course we are computers (unless substance dualism is true). We are physical beings, and we mean, or deal with meanings.

5. "Internal" Prospects

What lies ahead?

For discussion purposes, I will address this question using a distinction that is at the very least not black-and-white, and ultimately not one I believe in at all, but which will nevertheless bring some order to the discussion. I will divide my remarks into two categories: (i) "internal" prospects for working out the theoretical and scientific consequences of the views to which I argue, and (ii) more profound "external" implications, regarding our fundamental approach to metaphysics, ontology, and epistemology.

5a Internal

I said that computing involved a mixture of meaning and mechanism.[26] I also said that computer science uses a spate of terms borrowed from logic – including some (*identifier, symbol, reference, interpretation,* etc.) that, in logic, have squarely to do with semantics. It would be natural to suppose that these terms are used to describe the semantic or "meaningful" aspect of computing, rather than the "mechanism" side. Perversely, however, the converse turns out to be true. This is one reason why both Searle and his interpreters get confused. After recruiting semantical concepts (or at least terminology) from logic – terms or concepts that logic uses to analyse meaning – *computer science deployed them to study additional aspects of mechanism.*

How this came to pass is a complex story, but the result can be roughly caricatured. Computer science needed to understand the relation between a program, taken as a static or anyway passive entity that, plus or minus, both *describes* and *prescribes* a "computation," which for present purposes we can take to be the dynamic process that takes place when the program, as we put it, "runs." Because of the descriptive element, it was easy to parlay logic's notion of semantics to this purpose, since it took the form of mapping between one thing, "syntactic" or "grammatical" in form, and another, which logic had analysed in terms of a mathematical model. Logic's "semantic interpretation function" could thus be used, in computer science, to map programs onto the resulting processes, mathematically modeled or abstractly de-

---

[26] Admittedly, I haven't defended this statement—merely assumed it as the first dialectic. Given what is said in this and the next two paragraphs, it is not as simple a thesis to defend as one might expect, and so I will continue to do so here. See Smith (forthcoming).

scribed. Some work needed to be done. In order to capture the *prescriptive* part, for example, the interpretation relation needed to be constrained to be *effective* – in a way that would be perverse, if not outright unimaginable, in classical logic. From computer science's point of view, however, the move made sense. It is this restriction of interpretation to effectiveness that has spawned computer science's obsession with constructive mathematics, intuitionistic type theory, and eventually the development of linear logic, all in service of a kind of ultimately concretized meaning.

The problem with all this, however, is that the genuine semantical question, from a philosophical point of view, is not about the relation between program and process, but between process and world – between NASA's system to calculate trajectories and the *orbits of distant planets*, for example, or between the proximal results of NATO's early warning systems and the distal fact of whether an intercontinental missile strike *has in fact been launched*. Schematically, that is, we are faced with two relations connecting three realms: (i) between a program P and the process R that results from running it; and (ii) between that process R and the task domain D that the process is about, or that is the subject matter of the information that the process manipulates, or whatever. Computer science has used logic's semantical vocabulary to study the first relation, P⇒R, whereas the tough semantical question is about the second relation, R⇒D.[27] That remains to be theorized. (It is also a tough point to make to computer scientists, since you can't use any of logic's classic semantical concepts to describe it, as they have already all been "used up.")

One more technical result needs to be brought out. Earlier I mentioned debates about the "origin" of the computability limits first demonstrated by Turing, which form the foundations of computability and complexity theory. One of the results that emerges from the analysis of the effective computability (EC) construal is that recursion theory, the notion of computability, etc., turn out to be *mathematical models of physical constraint*. So that theory, too, is about the "mechanism" side of the substantive dialectic. It is framed as if it were a theory about the computation of numbers, but in fact it is a mathematical theory about reconfigurations of marks (i.e., of physically distinguishable states). This is obvious to programmers, increasingly recognized by computer scientists,

---

[27] As I once put it to Gordon Plotkin, a programming language semanticist, "I am interested in the semantics of the semantics of programs."

and anathema to logicians and recursion theorists. But no matter; it is again a tremendously positive result. The development of the theory of effective computability, once reconstructed as a mathematical theory of causation (below), is another intellectual achievement worthy of several trips to Oslo.

Given these understandings, I would identify the following four projects as the first half of my answer to Floridi's last question, about the most important issues facing the philosophy of computing. As I say, I see these four as "internal" to the subject matter. Even they are huge, and barely begun – but that just underlines what I said above: this is a new field, with most of the work remaining in front of us.

5a 1 – *Concretisation*

If computability and complexity theory is about mechanism and process, not numbers (cf. C4, above), then the entire theory must be recast in concrete terms. To take just one example, consider the infamous equivalence proofs discussed earlier. As currently cast, they claim that, if set up with appropriate inputs, one machine m_1 can "do the same thing" – that is, can "compute the same function" – as another m_2, if given the same input. As I said, that statement relies on a notion of "computing," which for two reasons must now be rejected. First, since 'compute' can no longer figure as a substantial property, we need to cleanse all theoretical statements of its use. Second, to the extent that there was any meaning to the phrasing "machine m computes function f," it is this: given "input" marks j denoting x, machine m can produce "output" marks k denoting $y=f(x)$. "Computing a function" has to do with mathematical entities – that is, with f, x, and y. On the recommended concrete overhaul, the theory would have to eschew all mention of such entities, and speak instead about machines and marks: m, j, and k.[28]

This transformation will be massive. Just one example: It is widely understood, and used to encrypt credit card numbers on the internet, that "factoring the products of two large primes" is a difficult task. But factoring is a phenomenon in the realm of *numbers*, not in the realm of *physical arrangements*. Moreover,

---

[28] The theory might (though I don't know whether it will) use functions and numbers to model or measure the concrete phenomena, in the way that physics uses numbers as a basis of measurement; but the resulting theory will no more be *about* numbers than to say that earth's escape velocity is 11,200 meters per second is a statement about the number 11,200.

factoring numbers is trivial if numbers are represented in non-standard ways – for example, as lists of their prime factors. So whatever is going on, "what is hard" must have to do with the nature of *numerals*. As such, it deserves framing in terms of marks, directly.[29]

I dub the recommended reconfiguration of the equivalence proof a motor theorem, with roughly the following content: Given a motor m_1, and an adequate stock of other passive but perfect parts,[30] one can assemble a configuration p of those parts, such that the resulting device, consisting of m_1 appropriately connected up to p – a device of potentially Rube-Goldberg complexity – will produce "isomorphic" behaviour, under a hugely broad metric of "equivalence," to that of any other machine m_2 that can be built.

Is the motor theorem impressive? Should we be impressed that such a theorem can be proved? Who knows? Personally, I should not have thought so.[31] Most concrete devices consist of some number of motors, gears, pulleys, containers, pipes, etc., or other forms of motive force. It does not seem to me especially odd that with one motor, of sufficient (that is: indeterminate) size, plus an indefinitely large supply of other perfect, friction-free parts (switches, ropes, pulleys, etc.) one could construct a device functionally isomorphic to any "perfect" device – especially if the metric of equivalence that one is mandated to meet, as in this case, is sufficiently broad. But normative assessment may be personal, and anyway should wait until much more of the reconstruction worked out in detail – something not yet done. The present point is simply that something like the motor theorem, plus appropriately detailed variants for all of the complexity variants, is mandated by the concrete understanding of the notion of "universality" that

---

[29] What kind of fact is that? It must have something to do with the composition of prime factorization with the inverse of the interpretation function for radix numerals—or rather that composition (or something like it) may play a role in its mathematical characterisation. But what that comes to, concretely—and why such an operation should be hard for a mechanism subject to our physical laws to perform—is going to take some work to figure out.

[30] Friction-free, totally discrete, and idealized in various other ways—these are the consequences or strictures of digitality, perhaps the most significant notion in the entire computational pantheon.

[31] I could never understand, when I first learned about the proofs of universal computability, why, in spite of their surface brilliance, I found them, *au fond*, to be so fundamentally boring. It took almost 20 years to figure out the answer.

comes out of this analysis.

In passing, one salutary effect of this "concretization" of our understanding of computation may be to help rid popular culture of various myths about computing, including the ubiquitous belief (false, in my view) that there is a fundamental distinction between the "virtual" world, on the one hand, and the "physical" or "real" one, on the other. Not only are computational processes (and worlds) *real*; they enjoy a materiality that, while different in tenor than that of our direct experience, is undergirded by the same physical laws and participates in the same temporality.[32]

5a 2 – Physical states

Another issue brought onto centre stage by the concrete reformulation of the mechanism side of computing is that of individuating physical states (or perhaps more correctly: physical state types). As Putnam points out,[33] one can claim that a rock implements any computation one wishes so long as one divvies up the physical states "appropriately" – which is to say, in completely unnatural ways. Deviant physical typing can produce lots of strange results: solving the halting problem, decrypting the most challenging encodings, solving traveling salesman problems in unit time. Of course, such Goodmanesque predicates[34] violate both intuition and utility. But what *is* an appropriate physical state? No one knows. All we can say is that an adequate theory of meaning and mechanism depends critically on the answer.

5a 3 – Process

"Computation," it used to be said, "is mathematics plus time." I disagree with the mathematics part, but the inclusion of temporality as computationally fundamental is unarguable. Process, doing things, what can happen, how long it takes – these are constitutive of the computational realm. Yet I think it is fair to say, almost a century after Husserl, Whitehead, and Heidegger, that we still do not have a theory of process and temporality worthy of the name. The temporally dependent variables of physics, enshrined in the

---

[32] Curiously, given contemporary processor speeds, the material worlds of computing manifest its relativistic character quite directly. It matters, if you are a thread running on a contemporary processor, that a nanosecond is approximately "equal" to a foot - in a way that doesn't enter our everyday phenomenology.

[33] Putnam H. (1991) *Representation and Reality*

[34] Such as Goodman's famous *grue* and *bleen*: green before some time *t*, and blue thereafter; and its converse.

calculus, are one spectacular success story, but they are extremely specific. There is no reason to believe that the "soul of a meaningful machine" will be disclosed through numerically valued measure properties.[35] By and large, computer science doesn't use them, instead analysing dynamic systems in terms of static structures – programs, inputs, outputs, requirements to be met, conditions to be honoured, contexts viewed as static abstractions. Why don't we deal with time more directly? As I continually ask graduate students, where is the programming language that is as natural for expressing jazz rhythms as Lisp is natural for expressing recursive functions? Should such a language *itself* be dynamic? Even in cases where we do employ mathematics, process and dynamics are modeled in terms of abstract a-temporal structures. Is the atemporality of mathematics a metaphysical, epistemological, or cognitive necessity? Is a dynamic mathematics[36] an unthinkable possibility?

History, I suspect, will laugh at us three times over: once for our reliance on objects, twice for the skittishness with which we approach relations, and three times for our naïveté about time.

5a 4 – Semantics

Finally, and most obviously, we need a theory of semantics – of the "meaning" side of that first substantive dialectic. In spite of the fact that essentially all of contemporary computer science's theoretical apparatus deals only with the mechanism side, it is not pure physicality that we are up against,[37] but, as I keep saying, meaningful mechanisms. Cognitive science recognizes the problem, e.g., in the so-called "symbol grounding" problem. But for an adequate intellectual understanding of semantics, intentionality, meaning, interpretation, reference, modeling, analysis, simulation, etc., we remain woefully in the dark.

It is on the semantic side of the equation that some look to the notion of information. The question is whether the "counter-

---

[35] Experience with computing to date suggests that architecture is a deeper analytic concept than measurement.

[36] Not just dynamic notation, nor a dynamic system about mathematics, nor a dynamic system mathematically modeled, but dynamic mathematics itself—such as sets changing membership over time, a hole opening up in a topological manifold, or an Abelian group's multiplicative operator losing its commutativity.

[37] Contra such writers as Phil Agre, who argue that computing is merely a practice of building physical stuff. See Agre P. (2002) The Practical Logic of Computer work in Scheutz M. (ed) *Computationalism: New Directions*

factual correlation" analysis of information content inaugurated by Dretske in 1981,[38] or perhaps the teleo-semantic variants developed since then, could be pressed into service for a genuinely semantic account of what information is, on which, in turn, a semantically grounded information-processing (IP) construal of computing could then rest. There are huge challenges to these accounts, involving such issues as how to deal with "misinformation" (if that is a species of information at all), avoid various forms of pan-informationalism, etc., but the effort is arguably the only substantial idea in town as to what a semantical account would actually look like.

My difficulty stems from two sources. First, as I will discuss more in a moment, I believe that extant accounts of information are fatally dependent on undischarged ontological assumptions, and therefore cannot serve as a basis for a thorough-going philosophical investigation. Second, however, and more immediately pertinently, I claimed that not all computing can be understood as "information processing," and therefore that the IP construal will not work as a general analysis (semantical or not). In a nutshell, the problem is that not all computing is *about* something else, as the notion of information would imply, but actually deals with things *in themselves*. When my email client tells me that I have new email, it does so by representing that fact (in English) in a window on my screen. When I go to retrieve the email, however, the computer *actually delivers it to me*; it does not merely provide me *information* about it. Should your message fail to arrive, it is not that I did not receive *information* about your communication. Rather, what is true is exactly what I say: "I did not *receive* it." Information-processing is not a strong or general enough notion to deal with the genuine encounter and engagement in our lives that computers and other meaningful mechanisms (like people) manifestly exhibit.

And so while I am as supportive as anyone of pursuing work in the philosophy of information,[39] and even teach a graduate seminar on the topic, I believe the vast reaches of an encompassing and adequate theory of the semantic dimension of meaningful mechanisms remain largely unexplored.

---

[38] *Knowledge and the Flow of Information*, 1981.

[39] Which is not to say that I believe that a theory of information is there to be found. We'll have to see.

6. "External" Prospects

Things are serious when (i) the "mechanism" side still needs theorizing, but we lack an account of physical types on which to base it; and (ii) the "meaning" side remains almost wholly unreconstructed. You might also think, since I have spent all these years struggling with the issues, that I would have something positive along these lines to propose.

In a way I do, but at best a cursory sketch. A hint of the reason is contained in the fact that we lack a theory of physical typing. After taking this long journey through the computational landscape, the most sobering result of all is to realise that the most serious problems to be addressed, in developing a theory of meaningful mechanisms, are *ontological,* not just mechanical or semantical. Even more seriously, the ontological issues involve an *inextricable mix* of mechanical and semantical concerns. Ontology, that is – by which I mean an ontological account of the entities necessary in order to give an account of computing and other meaningful mechanical systems – is inexorably tied into semantical or intentional or epistemological issues of meaning.

Space prohibits any real defense of this conclusion here, which is anyway too consequential to accept lightly – though the complexity of the subject matter revealed by a close look at all four dialectics may suggest some of the reasons. The magnitude of the impact, however, is not hard to see. Within traditional science and analytic philosophy, it is traditional to accept the following "division of labour": (i) to assume that the "ingredients" out of which an account will be constructed can be distinguished and identified in advance: the objects and properties and relations and sets and states of affairs and so forth; and then (ii) to develop the account of the meaning or semantics or epistemology in terms of them. Ontology, that is, is not only assumed to be separable from epistemology, but to precede it, in some logical or metaphysical sense. For example, if you were to write a computer program to control an elevator, you would first specify the world of elevators, floors, passengers, buttons, cables, etc., and then write the program *in such terms.* Requirements engineering pretty much assumes this.

The conclusion I have come to is that this approach will not work in the long run. As argued by legions of philosophers of a more literary stripe, ontology (what the world is like, in any intelligible sense) and epistemology (how we take the world to be) need to be reconstructed together. If we use 'metaphysics' to name that conjoined effort, then the answer to the original question about developing an adequate account of computing – i.e., as we can now see, a comprehensive theory of the meaning/mechanism dialectic – involves nothing less than a full-fledged assault on constructing an appropriate metaphysics.

So be it. For a bit more discussion, see Smith[40]; and for an inchoate stab at what such a metaphysics might look like, Smith (1996).[41]

In a way, the conclusion isn't surprising. Think about persistent online worlds – and the vexed questions that come up about whether avatars, into which people pour thousands of hours of devoted labour, are: (i) prostheses; (ii) beings in another reality; (iii) names or representations; (iv) identical to the player (warranting the common use of the term 'I' in such phrases as "I am going to slay the demon"), etc. Is a "crime" committed in such a world as innocuous as those investigated by Hercule Poirot, as serious as a "real-life" version, or something in between? And if the last, what existential or ontological conception of what is going on is strong enough to found such an ethical regime?[42]

What is striking is that ontological challenges aren't just "out at the level of use" – i.e., where people manifestly enter the picture. They permeate the entire subject matter. Even accounting for the identity conditions on a file outstrips the capacities of any known account. Is the file in the file cache, the one on the backup tape, the one I sent to you by email, the same? Or a copy? Sometimes it is convenient to think of it one way, sometimes the other. But is identity dependent on how we *think* of it? Maybe – but that's no innocent complication.

Similarly, any simple distinction between a sign and what is signified (name/named, description/described) is too blunt an instrument to deal with even simple computational systems. Does the ASCII version of a visual program *represent* the program, or *is it* the program, or is it a *translation* of the program? And what about the file I thought I lost, last night—but then realised that I didn't, because I had made a backup just a few hours before. Sure,

---

[40] Smith B. Varieties of Self-Reference, 1986, in Joseph Halpern, ed., *Theoretical Aspects of Reasoning about Knowledge*

[41] Note too the extent to this conclusion, wrung from an allegedly technical subject matter, resonates with claims made in feminist epistemology, science studies, and other poststructuralist initiatives. Not evidence for anything, exactly; but not sheer coincidence, either.

[42] See Kevin Eldred's forthcoming doctoral dissertation for an in-depth analysis.

I lost a few hours of editing—but still, I found "it." Says who? Says I. Which means that "the file," for me, is a singular term referring not to a particular physical copy, or even to a simple type of physical copy, or perhaps even to a more abstract single individual that the physical copy "realizes" (what's the difference between those two ways of putting it, anyway?), but to something yet more abstract – something whose identity conditions are more like the identity conditions on proofs we rely on to decide whether a young mathematician should be awarded tenure for their discovery of a "new proof" of a known result. In both cases, I would hazard, identity cannot be established independent of meaning – and perhaps even purpose. A sensible enough claim – but again a seriously expensive metaphysical result.

The problem, of course, is that once this gate is opened, and we take a step through, we enter a terrain of virtually unlimited grandeur and scope. The foundations of a great deal of what we consider science fall away, replaced by metaphysical and epistemological questions of almost unutterable consequence – and, needless to say, surpassing difficulty.

Objects, and in fact all of commonsense ontology, need naturalising, for starters – as much as any semantical or intentional notion. It isn't obvious where semantical or intentional notions will come from, either, since there won't yet be any stable ontology on top of which to build them. The semantic notion of information, for example, won't be able to speak of counterfactual dependencies between entities, at least not if it is going to play a foundational role on which those entities are going to depend. Or perhaps objects and information will arise together, with objects being patches of the world understood or "parsed" ("coarse-grained," as AI would put it) at a level or degree of abstraction that facilitates the kinds of counterfactual correlation that in turn allows us to track them. Who knows? It is not a crazy idea, even if how one would make good on it is not exactly obvious. It isn't just objects we need, either; the same goes for properties, relations, sets, etc. – to say nothing of "truth-makers" for non-conceptual content, be that Strawsonian feature-placings or whatever. Norms, too, or something to fill their role (perhaps fundamentally dynamic?) should be added to the list.

And so on. All I want to emphasise here, however, is the role of computation in this vast enterprise. For many years metaphysics has been viewed with huge suspicion – one of the few things on which both modernists and postmodernists agree. I am claiming, in contrast, that we are not going to understand computing – or meaning and mechanism more generally – unless and until we get over that suspicion, and take up the metaphysical gauntlet for real. Crucially, as I will argue elsewhere, that does not mean we need fall prey to any of the ways of doing metaphysics that have convinced a few centuries of philosophers that it is a hopeless and hapless enterprise. Interestingly, moreover, but consequentially, and something else that will need careful explanation, I believe that we can do so *empirically*, using computation as our laboratory – and not just metaphysics, but an indissoluble mixture of metaphysics, ontology, and epistemology; and not just theoretically, either, from an armchair or with Platonic detachment, but in an engaged, constructive, probably quite messy and concrete way.

Computers are not a subject matter, but as I said above, *laboratories of middling complexity* – vastly more complex than the atoms and frictionless pucks and pendula of simple mechanics, but vastly simpler than anything even reminiscent of human cognition. Whereas I identified four major challenges for future research "internal" to the study of computation, this is the one challenge – or rather, opportunity – I would name from the more serious and more sobering external perspective: that we recognize the first hundred years of computing as something of an Alchemical precursor to the intentional or meaningful sciences, and, with unswerving focus, parlay our computational experience into a finally successful metaphysics.

One final point, to bring the story full circle. The term 'material' is the adjectival form of 'matter' in both of its senses: 'matter' as a noun, as in "slurries are a form of matter studied by geologists"; and 'matter' as a verb, as in "it doesn't matter whether you call me or not." When we speak of *material objects*, most people assume we are using the form derived from the noun – that a *material object* is something that weighs something, that occupies space, that you might bump into. A material argument, however, of the sort a judge might deny you had raised, is of the other kind: an argument that *doesn't matter* (to whatever issue is at hand). How the two forms of 'matter' came apart could be argued, but suppose we lay it on Descartes. Then one way to describe the project laid out above is that of developing an understanding of a material object as a "spatio-temporal chunk of reality that matters"—thereby healing a temporary 300-year rift between *matter* and *mattering*.

And with that we can finally answer the questions with which I started. Can studying computing help us do to the richness and complexity of the human condition? Yes, but not in the way that I thought, back then. Computers can help by serving as a laboratory in terms of which to explore issues of intentionality, embodiment, semantics, meaning, mechanism, interpretation, etc., so long as we let go of the conceit that they are computers – or anyway, the conceit that their being computers is theoretically relevant. Can they be understood with all the power and insight and elegance of the sciences? Well, no – not if elegance requires formality. But formality has lost its sheen, for me at least, and I find more reward in exploring the metaphysical depths that these seemingly innocent devices have opened up in front of us. So yes, in a more grown up way – a way I just wasn't up to, at the time. Finally, as an added bonus, the time wasn't wholly "off" from physics, after all – as maybe my professor knew, and anyway is betrayed in the etymology. Maybe metaphysics is just physics, pushed harder. Hard enough to unleash meaning.

Time for second semester.

4

Gregory Chaitin

IBM Research Division

Yorktown Heights, USA

I consider myself to be a computer programmer who does mathematics as a hobby, a computer programming professional and amateur mathematician. I do not consider myself a philosopher. I have been forced to face some philosophical issues because of the kind of mathematics I do. And unlike a professional philosopher, I do not have an official position on every philosophical issue. I like to play with ideas: "On the one hand... On the other hand...," that sort of thing, some kind of an internal debate, never completely resolved.

Why was I initially drawn to computational and informational issues? As a child in the 1950s I read every issue of *Scientific American* from cover to cover, and kept a complete collection of these magazines in my room. Shannon's information theory had made quite a splash, and computer technology was progressing by leaps and bounds. I studied some of the earliest books on computer programming and computer technology, absolutely fascinated by these "thinking machines," these "giant electronic brains," as they were called then.

I also loved the clarity and sharpness of mathematical thought, which is the basis for physics, and read a lot of popularizations: W.W. Sawyer, G. Polya, Einstein and Infeld, E.T. Bell, G.H. Hardy, Tobias Dantzig, Courant and Robbins, endless piles of books from the New York Public Library.

And then I heard rumours that something was seriously amiss, that a crack had developed in the dike of mathematical thought, that there was a mysterious result questioning everything: Gödel's incompleteness theorem! It looked simple at first. It was all explained, very clearly, in a little book by Nagel and Newman called *Gödel's proof*, which I read and re-read.

However, the heart of the argument was a bizarre self-reference, "I am unprovable!," which made me very unhappy. It was as if you had asked the Delphic oracle for the secret of the universe, and it had responded, "43!" Perhaps correct, but not very enlightening. Could this be the mystery at the heart of understanding what mathematics was all about, what reasoning could or could not achieve?!

I **had** to understand this. The quest was intoxicating; I kept discovering fascinating new ideas.

Right away I discovered there was an approach to incompleteness that satisfied me far more than Gödel's proof. Turing's way of deducing incompleteness as a corollary of uncomputability seemed much more satisfying, much more solid and concrete. Computers and computer programs were quite tangible for me. I began learning the craft of computer programming as a teenager: machine language, assembly language, FORTRAN, recursive procedures, list processing, LISP, all that fun stuff, the carpentry of pure thought of the 20th century.

The most straightforward version of Turing's approach was in an article by S.C. Kleene in the *Encyclopaedia Britannica*: Let's define a **number-theoretic function** to be a function of a single argument, which is an un-signed integer, and which produces as its value, if there is one, another un-signed integer. Let $f_k(n)$ be the number-theoretic function calculated by the kth computer program, including the possibility that $f_k(n)$ is undefined because the computation doesn't terminate successfully. So sometimes these are partial, not total functions. Consider the number-theoretic function $F(n) = f_n(n) + 1$ if $f_n(n)$ is defined and 0 otherwise:

$$F(n) = \begin{cases} f_n(n) + 1 & \text{if } f_n(n) \text{ is defined} \\ 0 & \text{if } f_n(n) \text{ is not defined.} \end{cases}$$

Clearly F can't be one of the f_k, therefore F is uncomputable. Hence there can be no algorithm to decide if $f_n(n)$ is defined, therefore, following Turing, no formal axiomatic theory that enables you to prove whether $f_n(n)$ is defined or not in each particular case. For otherwise you could systematically run through the tree of all possible formal proofs and automatically decide whether or not $f_n(n)$ is defined, which would enable you to calculate the uncomputable function F!

This I could understand, this I could add to my intellectual toolkit. I immediately found an incompleteness theorem of my own. Let's imagine that we are using a formal axiomatic theory to prove that f_k, for specific, individual values of k, is a total function or isn't, whichever the case may be. Why can't we always do this?

First, let's forget about f_k, which includes partial functions. We'll use a different list of functions, g_k, all of which are total.

Consider a specific formal axiomatic theory in which it is possible to prove that a computer program computes a total number-theoretic function. Consider all the computer programs that **provably** compute a total number-theoretic function. List these programs in the order that such proofs are discovered as we systematically work our way through the tree of all possible formal proofs in our theory. This gives us a list g_k of all the computable number-theoretic functions which we can prove to be total in our theory. Now define $G(n)$ to be 2 raised to the maximum value of $g_k(n)$ for all k from 1 to n:

$$G(n) = 2^{[\max_{k=1}^{n} g_k(n)]}.$$

$G(n)$ is computable and it's a total number-theoretic function that goes to infinity with n much faster than any of the g_k functions. But g_k includes **all** the provably total computable number-theoretic functions in our formal axiomatic theory. Hence this theory cannot prove that the program for G computes a total number-theoretic function, even though it does. *Ipso facto*, we get incompleteness, and also a way to give an upper bound G on the power of a formal axiomatic theory using computational ideas.

Let's change topic. Fix the programming language for the entire discussion, and consider the **size** of a computer program, measured in bits of code. What if we want to show that we have the smallest computer program for a particular computational task, for example, the smallest computer program that computes a particular number-theoretic function? Let's call such a program **elegant**.

Can we do this?

Well, it's easy to see that any given formal axiomatic theory can only enable us to prove that finitely many specific, individual programs Π are elegant. And my proof of this gives us another way to measure, to bound, the power of a formal axiomatic theory, this time using the size in bits σ of the smallest computer program Θ that runs through all the proofs and generates all the theorems (a never-ending task). If we want to prove that a program is elegant which is substantially larger than σ, we will fail.

Why?

The proof, a *reductio ad absurdum*, is as follows. Consider the first provably elegant program Π that is larger than twice the size σ of Θ, the program for running through the proofs and finding all the theorems. I.e., Π appears in the first proof discovered by Θ that a specific program with size $\geq 2\sigma$ is elegant. Π is at least twice the size of Θ, but instead of using Π directly, we can instead take Θ, run it until it produces Π, and then run Π. This indirect way of getting Π reduces Π to half the size! And with more attention to technical details, and provided the programming language has certain suitable features, we can sharpen this result as follows: If a program Π is larger in size than the program Θ for producing all the theorems in our formal axiomatic theory, then this theory cannot enable us to prove that Π is elegant.

In more colourful language, if a program is larger than the complexity of a formal theory, then there is no way to prove that it's an elegant program within that theory. To prove that an n-bit program is elegant, you need an n-bit theory. Throughout this discussion – indeed, this entire essay – I make the implicit assumption that the formal axiomatic theory in question proves only true theorems.

Our constructions of F and G via diagonal arguments do in fact contain a self-reference, although a more palatable one than in Gödel's proof, namely when we look at $f_n(n)$ or $g_n(n)$. The unprovability-of-elegance proof that I have just given is genuinely different. It **is not** a diagonal argument, not even a concealed one. It's an information-theoretic argument.

The old idea of diagonal constructions, inspired by Cantor's diagonal argument in the theory of infinite sets, or in my case, actually, by Paul du Bois-Reymond's argument about orders of infinity that I read in a little book by G.H. Hardy, is replaced by something radically different. This is the idea of measuring the complexity of something by the size in bits of the smallest program for calculating it.

Let me give a more sophisticated illustration of these ideas. It involves the halting probability Ω, which is my version of Turing's famous halting problem, converted into a single real number Ω between 0 and 1 that is in fact the most compact oracle for solving the halting problem. If you were told the first n bits of the base-two binary expansion of the numerical value of Ω, that would in principle enable you to solve the halting problem for all programs up to n bits in size.

But the most interesting thing about Ω is not that it can serve as an oracle for the halting problem, it's the fact that the base-two bits of Ω are **irreducibly complex**. In other words, a program that computes n bits of Ω must itself be at least n bits in size. Furthermore, a formal axiomatic theory Θ that enables you to prove what are the first n bits of Ω (whether each bit is a 0 or is a 1) must itself have complexity n or more. In other words, the program for generating the theorems of Θ must be at least n bits long.

(*Caveat*: These statements depend on the appropriate choice of programming language for measuring program-size complexity, algorithmic information content or algorithmic complexity, whatever you may prefer to call it. The precise numerical value of Ω also depends on your choice of programming language. I shall not discuss any of this here.)

Right away, very concretely, the infinite stream of base-two bits of Ω shows that pure mathematics contains zones which are irreducibly complex. This example of irreducible complexity may seem a bit artificial, a bit contrived. However, the bits of Ω can be dressed up as statements about properties of diophantine equations or the word problem for semigroups, mathematical questions that on the face of it seem to have little to do with computation. *Immediate corollary*: Pure mathematics is infinitely complex and no finite set of axioms can fully exhaust it. In algebraic terms, the world of mathematical ideas has no finite basis.

As I learnt much later, the idea of irreducible complexity can be traced via Hermann Weyl back to Leibniz's 1686 *Discours de métaphysique*. And Vladimir Tasic points out that Emile Borel anticipated Ω, at least partially, with his 1927 know-it-all real number that can answer every possible yes/no question in French, by using the nth digit after the decimal point to answer the nth question.

Following the lead of Weyl and Tasic, I have studied the work of Leibniz and Borel and have done my best to advertise it and to make people appreciate how important it is. After all, Borel's 1927 number is extremely uncomputable, and this was a decade **before** Turing's famous paper "On computable numbers ..."

And we are immediately confronted with fundamental philosophical questions. In the case of Borel, ontological ones: Does his know-it-all real number really exist? Does Ω? Do real numbers exist? Can anything in the physical world be measured with infinite precision? Is physical reality continuous or discrete? Does any physical system contain an infinite number of bits of information? Does the entire universe? Zeno of Elea, all over again!

Even more important, through the connection with Leibniz, we are face to face with fundamental epistemological issues. What is a law of nature? Weyl expresses Leibniz's response to this question (*Discours*, Section VI) in a particularly dramatic fashion: If arbitrarily complex laws are permitted, then the concept of law becomes vacuous because there is always a law!

Let's restate this in terms of algorithmic information: A scientific theory is only of value to the extent that it's a compression. The number of bits in the theory (considered as software) must be substantially smaller than the number of bits of empirical data that we are trying to understand/explain. Understanding is compression of information; a good explanation is a good compression. (I am **not** discussing prediction.)

Furthermore, the best theory is the smallest computer program that reproduces exactly the empirical data. In other words, the best theory is what I've called an elegant program for calculating the experimental data. This permits us to quantify Leibniz's dictum (Section V of the *Discours*) that science is possible, that the world is comprehensible, precisely because God simultaneously minimizes the complexity of the laws of nature and maximizes the richness and diversity of the universe that these laws determine. In my toy model, both the laws of nature and the resulting universe are represented as a finite string of bits, and we merely compare their size. The laws are a program and the universe is its output.

What more can we do with these ideas, with this view of epistemology as information theory? It seems to me that viewed from this information-theoretic computational perspective, physical theories and mathematical theories are not that different. One is a compression of facts from the laboratory; the other compresses facts discovered with the aid of the computer, which is our laboratory when we do pure mathematics.

I have argued for many years that this provides support for what Imre Lakatos named a **quasi-empirical** view of mathematics, and that even if you are a firm believer in the reality of the Platonic world of mathematical ideas, you may sometimes have to add new, complicated, non-self-evident axioms to mathematics for pragmatic reasons, in order to be able to organize our mathematical experience better. Indeed, mathematicians, in working with the Riemann hypothesis, the hypothesis that $\mathbf{P} \neq \mathbf{NP}$, or the axiom of projective determinacy, are already behaving like physicists.

Most pure mathematicians, the true believers, the Platonists, will cry "heresy!" Materialist mathematicians may perhaps have some sympathy for my position, but they will deny the reality of Ω! I attempt to balance delicately between these two positions, having learned from Leibniz, whom I greatly admire, that some ideas are not as irreconcilable as most people think. Here is a completely different area where these ideas might apply. For many years I have hoped that perhaps the kind of complexity that I have been talking about in this essay has some kind of connection with biological complexity, and might eventually lead to a mathematical discussion of whether biogenesis and evolution are likely or not. I am thinking of an abstract model of life as software (our DNA!) that avoids getting into the messy details of molecular biology and biochemistry.

Furthermore, if mathematics is not static, if it is not a particular universal formal axiomatic system as Hilbert had hoped, then what is it? I would very much like to see a mathematical model of how mathematics evolves, of creativity, of how new ideas arise. Such a theory might also tell us how new biological ideas, new species, are created.

(A Platonist would phrase this differently: The world of pure mathematics, mathematical reality, is static, eternal and perfect. It is our imperfect and limited **knowledge** of this perfect world that is constantly evolving, constantly changing, and quasi-empirical.)

Clearly, much remains to be done; that is as far as I've been able to take these ideas so far. For more detailed discussions, see my non-technical book *Meta Math!*, the collection of my philosophical papers, *Thinking about Gödel & Turing*, or the *festschrift* Calude, *Randomness & Complexity, from Leibniz to Chaitin*.

There is also a U.K. edition of *Meta Math!* with a slightly different title, *Meta Maths*, and various translations into foreign languages are in progress.

The work on the word problem for semigroups that I referred to above is quite recent. My paper on this subject, "An algebraic characterization of the halting probability," will be published in volume 79 of *Fundamenta Informaticae*.

5

Daniel C. Dennett

Co-Director and Professor

Center for Cognitive Studies, Tufts University, USA

---

1. Why were you initially drawn to computational and/or informational issues?

When I was a graduate student in philosophy in Oxford in 1964, I encountered the little anthology edited by Alan Ross Anderson, called MINDS AND MACHINES (Prentice Hall, 1964). In it, were several now-classic essays: Turing's "Computing Machinery and Intelligence," Putnam's "Minds and Machines" (the first of his brilliant series of papers on functionalism) and Lucas' "Minds, Machines and Gödel", one of the earliest attempts to make the invited link between Gödel's theorem and the denial of physicalism (a forerunner of Penrose and others). Anderson was visiting England that year, and I invited him to speak to the Voltaire Society, of which I was then President. After his talk, he and I had a long discussion of the issues raised by these essays, and I was then sure I had to pursue them. The Feigenbaum and Feldman anthology COMPUTERS AND THOUGHT (1963) had Newell and Simon's classic essay "GPS, a Program that Simulates Human Thought," and other seminal papers by founders of AI. Feldman – Julian, not Jerome – was soon to be my colleague at UC Irvine in 1965, and he helped me find my way into the early literature of AI, and introduced me to Allen Newell and others – and asked for my help in rebutting a polemical piece that had just appeared as a RAND memo: Hubert Dreyfus's notorious "Alchemy and Artificial Intelligence," the ancestor of *What Computers Can't Do*. My first publication was a rebuttal of Dreyfus, published in the computer section of the journal *Behavioral Science*. I soon found myself in demand from the AI community as a philosopher who was sympathetic to AI, and able to explain its goals and prospects better, sometimes, than they could.

2. What example(s) from your work (or the work of others) best illustrates the fruitful use of a computational and/or informational approach for foundational researches and/or applications?

I think my essay "Artificial Intelligence as Philosophy and as Psychology" (1978) did a good job articulating and defending the research program of AI, and my rebuttal of Lucas, "The Abilities of Men and Machines" (1970), was an early anticipation of the rebuttals of Penrose and others who later tried to make illicit hay out of Gödel's theorem.

3. What is the proper role of computer science and/or information theory in relation to other disciplines, including other philosophical areas?

A point I have often made is that computer science keeps cognitive science honest. If it weren't for the practical possibility of constructing and demonstrating simplified working models of cognitive processes, we'd still be at the hand-waving stage. Ironically, it was the very difficulties encountered building scalable, realistically sized models that drove home the fact that cognition is much, much more complex than many theorists had realized. This has always been a contentious point, since it is always possible that the difficulties encountered are artifactual – owing to false enabling assumptions in the computer-modellers' kit – but although this is sometimes plausible, most of the good work in computer science (and related fields such as robotics) enlarges our appreciation for just how remarkable our brains are.

4. What do you consider the most neglected topics and/or contributions in late 20th century studies of computation and/or information?

The obvious problem is that we still have no solid theory of *semantic* information. Shannon-Weaver theory is excellent, but not a theory of content at all, and hence provides no answers to such straightforward questions as: what does *Romeo And Juliet* have in common with *West Side Story*? Or, how can a diagram or picture convey (mostly) the same information as a written description? We are "informavores," to use George Miller's vivid term, always eager to obtain more information about what matters most to us, and so, of course, we want lots of bits – but not useless bits. We want what the CIA calls "intelligence" on various topics. There is no good theory of semantic information so far as I know.

5. What are the most important open problems concerning computation and/or information and what are the prospects for progress?

The Frame Problem still looms large. How can a real time agent ignore the information that should be ignored while noticing both the changes and the constancies that demand its attention? That's not a formal expression of the problem, but it covers a range of issues that arise when one tries to make graceful use of world knowledge to generate relevant expectations about the future.

6

Keith Devlin

Executive Director and Senior Researcher

Center for the Study of Language and Information

Stanford University, USA

---

1. Why were you initially drawn to computational and/or informational issues?

In 1964, when a junior level high school student in Britain, I was fortunate to obtain a summer internship working at a nearby British Petroleum plant just after they purchased time on the first computer (an Elliott 803 mainframe) to be installed at the local university. (It was actually the first computer in the entire city.) Though my principal duty was initially data entry, I was totally intrigued by how the machine worked, and within a few weeks I had taught myself enough about *Algol*(the high level language the machine was equipped with) to be able to identify and fix a major flaw in the sales forecasting program the company was using. The following year BP hired me back for a second summer internship as a software developer, where I wrote a text editor for the on-site mainframe computer BP had just purchased, an Elliott Arch 9000, which came with a 9-instruction machine language and nothing else. (The instructions, called imaginatively using the digits 1 through 9, were all unary. It was pretty close to a Turing machine—and yes, input and output were by paper tape.)

Though the interest in computation this experience aroused in me never disappeared, it was overpowered by what I perceived to be (and I still think are) the far deeper intellectual challenges presented by mathematics, and I studied mathematics at university. It was only much later in my life, after spending many years as a university mathematician, that I began to look again at issues of computation. Having focused my research in mathematical logic, it was hardly surprising that my initial foray back into computation was in the area of artificial intelligence, but it was not long before I concluded that the original goal of "machines that think" was almost certainly not achievable (at least if those "machines" are digital computers), and my interest shifted to what I felt to be the more tractable, but still horrendously deep problem: what exactly *is* information?

I never did return to computing *per se*, either as practitioner or theorist, and accordingly this essay will focus almost entirely on information.

2. What example(s) from your work (or the work of others) best illustrates the fruitful use of a computational and/or informational approach for foundational researches and/or applications?

My first book about information, *Logic and Information*, published by Cambridge University Press in 1991, was based on Barwise and Perry's situation theory. (It actually began as a project to present their theory in a more mathematical fashion than they had in their earlier book *Situations and Attitudes*, published by MIT Press in 1983, but I ended up covering considerably more material, though in a less formal mathematical fashion than I had originally envisaged.) The focus of both books was on the use of situation theory to provide a framework for situation semantics, a theory of natural language semantics, that was particularly well-suited to capture, in particular, issues of indexicality.

Situation theory builds on our everyday, intuitive conception of information. This includes the kind of thing people seek when they approach an "information kiosk," perhaps by asking "Do you have any information about renting bicycles?" A number of ontological assumptions are required to get the theory off the ground. (In my answer to question 4, I'll explain some of the fundamental problems with the concept of information that motivated, in large part, the selection of the situation-theoretic ontology and the development of situation theory.)

First, we assume that information is in general distinct from its representation. Information is assumed to be a semantic concept (the representation being syntactic). We further assume that information is neither true nor false in of itself, but is made true by (or if you prefer, is true of) some part of the world — a *situation*. We write

$$s \models \sigma$$

to denote that the item of information σ is true in the context (i.e., situation) s.

Information is assumed to arise from (or be represented by) some configuration or event in the world by virtue of a *constraint*. Constraints can arise is various ways, from natural regularities (such as the constraint that dark skies are often followed by rain, and hence a dark sky provides the information that rain is likely), to conventions established by humans within a community (such as the convention that a bell ring in a school provides the information that class is over).

Formally, a constraint is defined to be a relation between two *situation types*. In turn, situation types are uniformities across situations. The "ringing bell indicates that the class is over" constraint would be a relation C between the type S of situation in which a bell rings and the type T of a class-ending (situation), written as

$$S \overset{C}{\Rightarrow} T$$

An agent who recognizes a situation s (say, audio input in the agent's current physical context, a linguistics class perhaps) to be of type S, written $s : S$, can infer that there is a situation t (perhaps the linguistics class) of type T, i.e., $t : T$.

A formal calculus of informational entities (*infons*), situation types, and constraints makes it possible to develop these ideas to a point where they can be applied to analyze linguistic utterances and information flow, and situation *semantics* met with some initial success. But the real descriptive/analytic power of situation *theory* was not realized until Duska Rosenberg and I applied it to analyze linguistic data gathered in the course of an ethnographic study of workplace communication.

In our monograph *Language at Work – Analyzing Communication Breakdown in the Workplace to Inform Systems Design*, published by CSLI Publications in 1996, Rosenberg and I used situation theory to organize the ethnographic data Rosenberg had collected in a lengthy workplace study. Our approach was inspired by an analytic approach to language developed by the ethnomethodologist Harvey Sacks. Based on Sacks' work, we created an analytic methodology called Layered Formalism and Zooming (LFZ analysis), and that was what we used to analyze the data collected from the ethnographic study. Our analysis led to specific, implementable recommendations to the company for increasing efficiency.

The key to our success was that, although situation-theoretic descriptions and analyses of linguistic communication are, in all but extremely simple, "toy" examples, nothing like as precise as the mathematical descriptions and analyses employed in, say, physics, they nevertheless prove to be very effective in bringing an unprecedented degree of mathematical precision to the analysis of everyday human–human communication from a social science perspective. In short, situation theory turned out to be ideally suited for bringing greater formality to analyses of complex sociolinguistic data.

While I believe that our monograph did make fundamental scientific contributions to our understanding of information, its greatest initial impact was through the practical application that was the primary focus of our study. Several industrialists expressed interest in the work, but a common complaint was that our account was too heavily mathematical, which for many potential readers made it inaccessible. Accordingly, a short while later I brought out another book on the topic aimed squarely at the business community, called *Infosense*. In that account, I reduced the mathematical formalisms to an absolute minimum, and provided many examples from everyday life.

3. What is the proper role of computer science and/or information theory in relation to other disciplines, including other philosophical areas?

I don't agree with the unstated assumption behind this question. I do not think there is such a thing as a "proper role." Terms I would agree with are "useful role" or "appropriate role." Science is about understanding and engineering is about building, and whatever helps either is justifiable. For example, Stephen Wolfram has been promoting the idea of natural science based on computation (his "a new kind of science"). As it happens, I don't think that the approach he outlines in his book by that name succeeds as a viable alternative to current (property/relation-based) science, but that is because of his particular approach, not because I think there is a philosophically preferred framework for doing science.

Earlier in my career I would have answered this question differently. Academics are in the business of acquiring and disseminating knowledge. To do this in a systematic way requires an epistemic framework, and that framework governs practically everything a professional in a particular academic discipline does. In the case of the discipline (or disciplines, if you carve things more finely) generally referred to as "Foundations of Mathematics," there is an innate linear ordering — or perhaps a tree — that attempts to impose (or reflect) an order in which one concept is built on another. Thus, the notions of a formal logic and an abstract set are often taken as basic, axioms for both are introduced, and structures such as the natural numbers and the higher number systems are built up within set theory. This viewpoint carries with it, for those who pursue foundational studies, a sense of being "the way things are," or even more strongly, "the way things have to be." Moreover, because the foundations of mathematics is almost universally viewed and practiced as a *synthetic* discipline, practitioners frequently develop a sense that the theory is *prior* to any applications, particularly applications in the real world. Indeed, the very use of the term "applications" reflects this viewpoint.

An alternative approach is to take the world as we encounter it, both the physical world and the social world, and regard the various academic frameworks as simplifying filters that aid our understanding and facilitate analysis. For much of my career, I had the former view; of late I have aggresively adopted the latter. From this "materially pragmatic" perspective, there are no "proper" frameworks; the only metric is efficacy.

From this perspective, what we call "foundational studies" are a finer-grained *analysis* of the epistemically-prior mathematical framework we use to study and understand the world, and the "foundations of mathematics" are not foundations in the sense of the foundations of a building, they are more like the roof. Interestingly, I believe this is precisely the view that the vast majority of mainstream mathematicians always had of foundational studies. For instance, most mathematicians were not the least bit phased by Gödel's Incompleteness Theorems or by Cohen's undecidability results in set theory, which they viewed as dealing with the icing on the top of the cake rather than something truly foundational on which their own work depended. My present philosophy simply extends this view from foundational studies to all of mathematics.

4. What do you consider the most neglected topics and/or contributions in late 20th century studies of computation and/or information?

I'll concentrate entirely on information, since this is what my work has mostly focused on.

I think that it took far too long a time before theorists began to recognize the fundamental problems associated with the notion of information, and to view information as a social construct. (Many still do not.) In particular, Shannon and Weaver's use of the term "information theory" to describe their quantitative, entropy-based approach to communication delayed the development of genuine "*information* theories" considerably. For one thing, the real focus of their theory was a (highly useful) notion of channel capacity, measured in bits, not on information as most people commonly use that word, which is to refer to the "information" that those bits carry. Put simply, counting bits in a signal tells you almost nothing about the information (i.e., what a person would typically call "information") that the signal may carry, which depends entirely on contextual factors. To take a simple example, two people can establish a convention whereby a signal of a single bit can carry an enormous amount of information. Admittedly, the Shannon-Weaver theory can handle this, by considering the convention as part of the system, and this can be philosophically justified, but to my mind the result is unsatisfyingly contrived, and not at all as mathematically crisp as their framework suggests.

A more appropriate approach, I believe, is to start with the everyday notion of information, make that as precise as possible, and then proceed to analyze the way that information arises, is stored, and is transmitted. This is precisely the approach adopted by situation theory, as outlined above. (It is also, of course, consistent with my overall philosophy of mathematics as outlined in the previous section.)

It is when you approach information in an analytic fashion that you soon find yourself mired in complexity. For instance, at first blush, if I come up to you and say "I just won a major award for my paper on information," and someone were then to ask you what information my statement conveyed to you, almost certainly you would say "Devlin just won an award for a paper he wrote on information." You are less likely to give any of the following replies:

- "Devlin speaks English with a Yorkshire accent."

- "The man who just spoke to me is alive."

- "The man who just spoke to me was nervous."

- "The man who just spoke to me was lying."

- "The man who just spoke to me was intoxicated."

Yet my utterance could equally have conveyed each of those other pieces of information, depending on the circumstances. (It would always convey the information about my accent and the information about my being alive.) Indeed, under the appropriate circumstances, any one of those alternative pieces of information, and an endless sequence of further possibilities, could be said to be the *primary* item of information you, as listener, acquired from my utterance. (Consider immigration officials at airports, who often ask a returning passenger "What was the purpose of your trip?" The official couldn't care less what you were doing, he or she simply wants to see if you display any signs of unusual nervousness that might indicate a problem. In this situation, the key information being sought, and often obtained, is not encoded in what you say, but how you say it.)

In fact, by taking advantage of, or establishing, the appropriate circumstances, practically any signal can be used to store and convey any piece of information, the famous knotted handkerchief being a familiar everyday example of a one-bit representation that can mean one thing one day, another thing the next.

Once you recognize that information depends fundamentally on the circumstances — that words, objects, actions, etc. can convey pretty well any information we want them to — you have to admit that a study of information has to be carried out in a framework that captures enough of the social context in which it arises, is transmitted, and is consumed. How much is "enough" in that last sentence? That was one of the questions the early developers of situation theory had to address. I always felt they did a pretty good job for the first pass — which is why I decided to throw my lot in with the situation theory camp not long after they got their theory off the ground, in the early 1980s.

5. What are the most important open problems concerning computation and/or information and what are the prospects for progress?

The end of my response to question 4 provides my answer to this question. Although there have been a number of attempts to develop formal theories of information (in the everyday sense of the word "information"), to my mind, none have truly succeeded. I believe there is considerable scope for advancement in this area, but it has to be accepted from the start that, since information (as understood by most people, and as I approach it) is a social construct, there is no possibility of developing formal, mathematical theories that resemble, say, classical logic. I believe formality and mathematical precision can be best (and possibly only) achieved through a zooming methodology of the kind Rosenberg and I describe in our monograph.

Such an approach is very different from the currently-accepted conception of mathematical formality, which seeks to provide a (ground-level) formal theory. Instead, the formality lies in the *process* used in an endless *activity* of analysis.

Such a development would be an instance of what I believe will be a general shift in the way we bring mathematics to bear in analyzing social issues. Seduced — with very good reason, I may add — by over two millennia of incredible success in developing and using mathematics to understand the physical world, we came to accept the way mathematics works its magic, with depth, precision, formality, and finality. It was, and remains, the case that when we try to apply mathematics in the social realm, however, things do not work out anything like as well, and attempts to emulate physics in the study of social concepts such as information are doomed to fail.

Economists recognized this long ago, and now make sophisticated use of the latest mathematical models *along with other forms of reasoning that cannot be captured in an equation*. A similar appreciation of the limits of mathematics has yet to be realized by — to pick on just one particular group by way of example — many in the artificial intelligence community, who still purport to believe in a future, mathematically-specified, (digital-) machine intelligence that will equal or surpass the human mind. (You will gather that I do not share that view. I explained my reasons at length in my book *Goodbye Descartes*, so will not repeat here what I wrote there. Many others have articulated similar objections to GOFAI – "Good Old-Fashioned Artificial Intelligence". I should perhaps add that I have always been impressed by some of the real advances in software systems made under the banner of "AI"; it is the original bold goal of GOFAI that I object to.)

Part of the lesson that must be learned in order for new mathematics to be developed that will enable us to truly gain better understanding of social issues such as information, is that rigor does not require mathematical formalism (axioms, formal proofs, and the like). Moreover, when it comes to understanding many social phenomena, the goal is not "perfect understanding" but "better (i.e., deeper, more precise, more illuminating, more useful) understanding."

To take just one example of many possible, Chomsky's mathematical theory of *syntactic structure*, first outlined in his famous 1957 book by that title, provided a mathematical formal description of certain important features of sentence structure. We learned a great deal about language by virtue of Chomsky's mathematics. Not because his theory captured language the way the atomic theory of matter captured (or modeled, if you prefer) the material world around us. It most obviously did not do that. Rather, we learned more about language by seeing the *extent* to which real language both *conforms to* and *differs from* Chomsky's mathematical descriptions.

A second example that comes to mind is Paul Grice's "maxims of everyday language usage,"[1] where he adopts a decidedly Euclid-like axiomatic approach to explaining how people use language to communicate. In the case of Chomsky, the mathematics actually *looks like* (symbolic) math; Grice's work, in contrast, does not easily lend itself to symbolic presentation, yet his approach is clearly "mathematical".

Both Chomsky's work on syntax and Grice's observations on communication are examples of what I am convinced will be a growing trend of using a mathematical or mathematically-inspired approach to increase our understanding of social phenomena. My work with Rosenberg cited earlier falls into the same category.

I believe that the 21st century will see considerable progress in understanding information in this vein, but I suspect that the majority of scholars currently active in "foundational studies" would not, were they to live long enough, recognize or endorse such work as "of their own". Rather, what will transpire, I foresee, is yet another instance of the oft-cited observation of Max Planck that a new scientific paradigm comes to ascendency not because the new turks convince the old guard, rather that the old guard simply die off.

Whether the new guard will refer to such work as "mathematics" I would not hazard a guess, and I don't think it really matters. Whatever it is called, it will give us a greater understanding of information, how it arises, how it is transmitted, and how to process it.

---

[1] See his paper "Logic and conversation", available in Cole, P. and Morgan, J. (eds.) *Syntax and Semantics, Vol 3* New York: Academic Press, and also downloadable from several websites.

7

Fred Dretske

Senior Research Scholar

Department of Philosophy, Duke University, USA

Information, Computation and Cognition

I have spent much of my professional life worrying about epistemological problems: what do we know and how do we know it?
Answering these questions requires a reasonably developed view
about what knowledge is. During the early part of my career,
then, I spent a lot of time thinking about perception, one of our
most important sources of knowledge (some philosophers regard
it as our *only* source of knowledge). What is it that perception
gives and how does it give it? In (Dretske 1969) I reached answers
to these questions that have, in one form or another, remained
with me ever since. As often happens in philosophy, though, there
were technical problems with (aka troubling objections to) my answers. In struggling with these problems, my attention was called
(by Ken Sayre in conversation and also Sayre 1965) to Shannon's
mathematical theory of information (Shannon 1948). Although I
did not agree with Sayre's particular use of the theory, I thought
he was on the right (at least a promising) track in deploying the
machinery of communication theory to the study of knowledge
and related epistemological ideas. Shannon's theory, what little I
knew of it at the time, seemed ideally suited to help me with my
problems.

Information, at least as it is commonly understood, is, after all,
an epistemologically important commodity. One needs – either by
direct perception, testimony, books, newscasts, or other means –
information in order to know. Without information one remains ig-
norant. So, since knowledge is important, so is information. That,
surely, is why so much money is spent on the collection, storage,
and retrieval of information. That, surely, is why we, in our practical lives, rely on accredited sources of information (timetables,

schedules, guide books) in making travel plans. It is why we read
the newspapers, watch the evening news, and seek advice from
experts. It is why, during wartime, people are willing to kill to
get it and die to conceal it. We very much want to know and,
sometimes, very much want others not to know. So we value the
information needed to know.

So if Shannon could tell me what information was, or if not information, then at least the conditions of a communication channel
that made possible its transmission, then Shannon could tell me
something philosophically important. His formulae for measuring
the efficiency of a communication channel, something he called
the amount of mutual information between source and receiver,
was, it seemed to me, a means for expressing the conditions that
I thought had to exist between knower (at a receiver) and known
(events occurring at a source) for knowledge of these events to be
possible. What I had been trying to say in *Seeing and Knowing*
(1969) and later (Dretske 1971) about the kind of connection that
had to exist between perceiver and perceived, between knower and
known, in order for knowledge to be possible could, perhaps, now
be said more perspicuously and convincingly with the terminology and formulae of communication theory. Doing so might also,
as a side benefit, encourage useful exchanges between epistemology and cognitive science.

Such was the project in (Dretske 1981) – *Knowledge and the
Flow of Information*. One problem, though, was immediately evident. Shannon's formulae expressing the mutual information between source and receiver were formulae that expressed weighted
averages of conditional probabilities of *all* the events that might
occur at these points. These quantities were of interest to an engineer thinking about the best way to code information transmitted over a channel connecting these points, but they were of little
use to a philosopher concerned with knowledge. Knowledge, at
least perceptual knowledge, is usually knowledge of some particular event occurring at a particular place and time: that the stock
market fell today, that Billy is still at home, that her telephone
number is 471-3489. Whatever channel one uses to obtain information about these matters, the average reliability of the channel
seems to be quite irrelevant. For example, since Jimmy has a dis-
tinctive look and manner, I can know it is him when I spot him
leaving the bank, even though I could not, at this distance and
dim light, have identified anyone else. The "signal" that carries information to me – the light reflected from Jimmy – is good enough

to give me knowledge of who it is, even though this information (that it is Jimmy) arrives over a channel that is (from the point of view of communication theory) a very noisy channel. Nine times out of ten (in these poor viewing conditions), one would be wrong about who it was leaving the bank. The set of conditional probabilities defining noise and equivocation – and, therefore, Shannon's mutual information between the source (person leaving the bank) and receiver (me) – can be almost anything without precluding knowledge of the source on a particular occasion.

So, if I was going to use Shannon to help me with Descartes and Kant, the application wasn't going to be straightforward. There would have to be some cutting and pasting, some pushing and pulling, to make informational concepts do work they weren't (in communication theory) designed to do. This wouldn't have been a surprise to Shannon. He (and Weaver in his contribution to Shannon and Weaver 1949) didn't think that what the quantity engineers and mathematicians were talking about had much, if anything, to do with information as ordinarily understood.[1] Information, as ordinarily understood, is a creature of semantics, not statistics. It may be possible to define a measure of the communicational effectiveness of a connection (channel) linking source and receiver in bits, but information itself doesn't come in these units. The information carried by a light reflected from Jimmy is that the person leaving the bank is Jimmy. We can, if we like, define a measure of how much information this fact – that it is Jimmy – represents (e.g., 1 kilobyte), but the information itself – that it is Jimmy – is clearly not the same as the information that the person leaving the bank is Bobby, even if both pieces of information have exactly the same measure. What is important in a theory of knowledge is not *how much* information is transmitted – 1 byte or 1 gigabyte – but *what* information. Was it Jimmy or Bobby?

This is simply to say that information, as ordinarily understood,

---

[1] Shannon (p. 3: Shannon and Weaver 1949): "These semantic aspects of communication are irrelevant to the engineering problem." Weaver (p. 99 in Shannon and Weaver 1949): The word *information* in this theory is used in a special sense that must not be confused with its ordinary usage. In particular, *information* must not be confused with meaning." Although Weaver thinks Shannon's theory applies, in the first instance, to the technical (engineering) aspects of communication (how to efficiently transmit symbols from place to place), he thinks that it is also helpful and suggestive for understanding the semantic aspects of communication (see p. 114). With this I fully agree.

is a *semantic*, not a statistical, commodity. It is always *about* something. It has a topic, what it is information about. You get information about the stock market from the newspapers, about the war in Iraq from the television news, about the planet Venus from a book on astronomy, and about the patient's aorta from an ultrasound. Information has what philosophers call *intentionality*. Information, however, is not only about some topic. What it says about this topic must be *true* in order to qualify as information. That, I submit, is the reason information is important. If information did not have to be true to be information, why would anyone want it? Why would anyone need it? Why would anyone care about it? We want (need, care about) information because of our desire or need to know, and knowledge requires truth. That is why you can't know (believe, yes, but not know) that pigs can fly. It just isn't true that pigs can fly. That is why an announcement by the highest authority that pigs can fly fails to carry the information that pigs can fly. You can, to be sure, enter this "fact" about pigs into a computer's data base (or a person's brain), but putting it there and letting the computer (whether machine or human brain) operate on it as if it were true doesn't make it true. It doesn't make it information. You can cause people to believe it, yes, but you can't cause them to know it.

We sometimes talk about misinformation, disinformation, and false information. This leads some people to conclude, mistakenly, that information needn't be true. The reasoning seems to be that since false information is information and it is clearly not true, information needn't be true. This is a pretty heavy-handed treatment of ordinary language. It is like concluding that not all ducks are animals because decoy ducks aren't animals. The right conclusion to draw from the existence of decoy ducks, of course, is not that ducks need not be animals, but that decoy ducks aren't ducks. Likewise, the proper conclusion to draw from the existence of false information is not that information needn't be true. It is, rather, that false information is not information. False teeth aren't real teeth; why should false information be real information? False information is *fake* information and fake information is not a species of information any more than fake diamonds are a kind of diamond or phony dollar bills are (real) dollar bills.

The fact that information must be true in order to be information is why people whose primary interest is computation (computer scientists, software designers, and communication engineers), aren't much interested in information. Computation, by its nature, is blind to the feature (truth) that makes something information. Garbage can be processed as efficiently as information as long as the garbage exhibits the formal properties over which computational routines are performed. Logicians (qua logicians), for instance, don't care whether premises are true. They are interested in validity – symbol manipulations that *preserve* truth. One can, however, have a flawless procedure for preserving truth, a perfect validity machine, and never come within shouting distance of a truth. Truth doesn't matter. The computations are the same whether operations are performed on truths or falsehoods.

The fact that computers cannot distinguish garbage (meaningless strings of symbols) from information doesn't mean that garbage *is* information. All it means is that computational processes – those occurring in computers as well as brains – cannot distinguish garbage from information. It is important, nonetheless, to insist on the distinction between computation and information. It is important, not only to philosophy, but to cognitive science in general. For cognition is not just a matter of impeccable reasoning and flawless inference. It is not just a matter of computational excellence. It is also a matter of getting things right (is that a tiger or a zebra in the bushes, a stick or a snake in the grass), and getting things right is something that requires, besides computational excellence, information. Truth. We not only have brains, we have eyes and ears, and although it may be the job of the brain to compute – to figure out from scanty input, what is in the bushes – it is the job of the senses to provide the information over which these computations are performed so as to yield true conclusions about what is there.

I harp about these verbal issues because, I suspect, contributors to this volume will be using the term "information" in many different ways, and I want to be clear about how I am using it. I am talking about: (1) a semantic entity. Information is about something. It has a topic. And it says something about this topic. This is what enables information to have the second key property: (2) information is true. This, as far as I can see, is why information is important. Why it is valued. And (3) information is transmissible from one place to another. It can be sent from world to brain (e.g., perception), from brain to brain (communication), and from machine (computer, cell phone, etc.) to machine (information technology). This, indeed, is why information is useful. It can be shared. So if we want a theory of information, this, I assume, is what we want a theory of. We want an account of what confers on physical events the power, the capacity, to carry something that has these three properties.

If, as I (once again) suspect, contributors to this volume mean something else by the term "information" then our answers to the questions posed will not only be different, they will be different *because* – and, perhaps, *only* because – they are (understood to be) answers to quite different questions. This, I think, is a danger to be kept in mind in evaluating the answers. The disagreements – and there are sure to be many – might not run very deep once the merely verbal differences are sorted out.

I have only one closing observation to make. This is related to the final question – open problems about information? – in the set of five questions to which this essay is a response. The lack of information, the absence of information that so-and-so happened, is not to be confused with the information that so-and-so didn't happen. Only in very special circumstances does the absence of positive information (that P is true) constitute negative information (that P is false). These are circumstances in which through prior arrangement or a special situation one would have heard if so-and-so happened. Not hearing, then, is information that it didn't happen. Not hearing from my wife doesn't tell me anything about her unless she tells me (or we have an understanding) that she will call if she needs a ride. In that case, not hearing from her constitutes information that she doesn't need a ride. Without this prior understanding, though, her failure to call is not information one way or the other.

Obvious as this distinction is, information technology tends to conceal a growing danger to its proper application in online research. In our increasing reliance on computers to gather information, we may forget that there are many reasons why information, though accessible in other ways, may not be available online. It may not (yet) have been digitized (it is estimated that despite ambitious digitization efforts at the U.S. Library of Congress, only about 10% of its vast collection will be digitized anytime soon). There may be copyright restrictions that prevent its online accessibility. The information may appear in materials that cannot (because of delicacy of manuscripts, odd size of publication, etc.) easily be converted to digital form. Thus, a complete lack of online information that so-and-so happened may or may not be information that so-and-so didn't happen. It depends. It depends on whether such information would be available online if so-and-so really happened. That may not always be clear. Sometimes it is clearly not so. It is important to know which is which. An automatic (and, therefore, careless) assumption that it is always true is tantamount to elevating ignorance (that something happened) to the status of knowledge (that it didn't). The New York Times (March 11, 2007) warns that as computers become the main tool of research, items left in non-digital form may begin disappearing from our collective memory. That is a danger, of course, but even more dangerous is the possibility that, because of mistaken assumptions about what information is actually available online, facts are not only removed from collective memory, they are replaced by their denials.

References

Dretske, F. 1969. *Seeing and Knowing.* Chicago: University of Chicago Press.

Dretske, F. 1971. Conclusive Reasons, *Australasian Journal of Philosophy* (May).

Dretske, F. 1981. *Knowledge and the Flow of Information.* Cambridge: MIT Press (A Bradford Book).

Sayre, K. 1965. *Recognition: A Study in the Philosophy of Artificial Intelligence.* South Bend: University of Notre Dame Press.

Shannon, C. 1948. The Mathematical Theory of Communication. *Bell System Technical Journal,* July and October.

Shannon, C. and Weaver, W. 1949. *The Mathematical Theory of Information.* Urbana: University of Illinois Press.

8

Hubert L. Dreyfus

Professor of Philosophy

University of California, Berkeley, USA

---

1. Why were you initially drawn to computational and/or informational issues?

When I was teaching at MIT in the early sixties, students from the Artificial Intelligence Laboratory would come to my Heidegger course and say in effect: "You philosophers have been reflecting in your armchairs for over 2000 years and you still don't understand how the mind works. We in the AI lab have taken over and are succeeding where you philosophers have failed. We are now programming computers to exhibit human intelligence: to solve problems, to understand natural language, to perceive, and to learn." In 1968 Marvin Minsky, head of the AI lab, proclaimed: "Within a generation we will have intelligent computers like HAL in the film, 2001."

As luck would have it, in 1963, I was invited by the RAND Corporation to evaluate the pioneering work of Alan Newell and Herbert Simon in a new field called Cognitive Simulation (CS). Newell and Simon claimed that both digital computers and the human mind could be understood as *physical symbol systems*, using strings of bits or streams of neuron pulses as symbols representing the external world. Intelligence, they claimed, merely required making the appropriate inferences from these internal representations. As they put it: "A physical symbol system has the necessary and sufficient means for general intelligent action."

As I studied the RAND papers and memos, I found to my surprise that, far from replacing philosophy, the pioneers in CS had learned a lot, directly and indirectly from the philosophers. They had taken over Hobbes' claim that reasoning was calculating, Descartes' mental representations, Leibniz's idea of a "universal characteristic" – a set of primitives in which all knowledge could be expressed, Kant's claim that concepts were rules, Frege's formalization of such rules, and Russell's postulation of logical atoms as the building blocks of reality. In short, without realizing it, AI researchers were hard at work turning rationalist philosophy into a research program.

At the same time, I began to suspect that the critical insights formulated in existentialist armchairs, especially Heidegger's and Merleau-Ponty's, were bad news for those working in AI laboratories – that, by combining rationalism, representationalism, conceptualism, formalism, and logical atomism into a research program, AI researchers had condemned their enterprise to re-enact a failure.

Using Martin Heidegger and Maurice Merleau-Ponty as guides, I began to look for signs that the whole AI research program was degenerating. I was particularly struck by the fact that, among other troubles, researchers were running up against the problem of representing significance and relevance – a problem that Heidegger saw was implicit in Descartes' understanding of the world as a set of meaningless facts to which the mind assigned what Descartes called values, and John Searle now calls functions.

But, Heidegger warned, values are just more meaningless facts. To say a hammer has the function of being for hammering leaves out the defining relation of hammers to nails and other equipment, to the point of building things, and to the skills required when actually using the hammer – all of which reveal the way of being of the hammer which Heidegger called *readiness-to-hand*. Merely assigning formal function predicates to brute facts such as hammers couldn't capture the hammer's way of being nor the meaningful organization of the everyday world in which hammering has its place.

Minsky, unaware of Heidegger's critique, was convinced that representing a few million facts about objects, including their functions, would solve what had come to be called the common-sense knowledge problem. It seemed to me, however, that the deep problem wasn't storing millions of facts; it was knowing which facts were relevant in any given situation. One version of this relevance problem was called "the Frame Problem." If the computer is running a representation of the current state of the world and something in the world changes, how does the program determine which of its represented facts can be assumed to have stayed the same, and which would have to be updated?

Minsky suggested that, to avoid the Frame Problem, AI programmers could use what he called frames – descriptions of typical situations like going to a birthday party – to list and organize those, and only those, facts that were normally relevant. But a system of frames isn't *in* a situation, so in order to select the possibly relevant facts in the current situation one would need frames for recognizing situations like birthday parties, and for telling them from other situations such as ordering in a restaurant. But how, I wondered, could the computer select from the supposed millions of frames in its memory, the relevant frame for selecting the birthday party frame as the relevant frame, so as to see the current relevance of, say, an exchange of gifts rather than money? It seemed obvious to me that any AI program using frames to organize millions of meaningless facts, so as to retrieve the currently relevant ones, was going to be caught in a regress of frames for recognizing relevant frames for recognizing relevant facts, and that, therefore, the Frame Problem wasn't just a problem but was a sign that something was seriously wrong with the whole approach.

Unfortunately, what has always distinguished AI research from a science is its refusal to face up to and learn from its failures. In the case of the relevance problem, the AI programmers at MIT in the sixties and early seventies limited their programs to what they called micro-worlds – artificial situations in which the small number of features that were possibly relevant was determined beforehand. Since this approach obviously avoided rather than solved the real-world Frame Problem, MIT PhD students were compelled to claim in their theses that their micro-worlds could be made more realistic, and that the techniques they introduced could be generalized to cover commonsense knowledge. There were, however, no successful follow-ups.

2. What example(s) from your work (or the work of others) best illustrates the fruitful use of a computational and/or informational approach for foundational researches and/or applications?

In March 1986, several graduate students at the MIT AI lab. invited me to give a talk. I called the talk: "Why AI Researchers should study *Being and Time*." In my talk I repeated my Heideggerian critique of representationalism from *What Computers Can't Do*: "[T]he meaningful objects ... among which we live are not a *model* of the world stored in our mind or brain; *they are the world itself.*" And I quoted approvingly a Stanford Research Institute report that, "It turned out to be very difficult to reproduce

in an internal representation for a computer the necessary richness of environment that would give rise to interesting behavior
by a highly adaptive robot," and concluded that "this problem is
avoided by human beings because their model of the world is the
world itself."

The year of my talk, Rodney Brooks, who had moved from
Stanford to MIT, published a paper criticizing the idea that robots should use representations of the world and problem solving
techniques to plan their movements. He reported that, based on
the idea that "the best model of the world is the world itself," he
had "developed a different approach in which a mobile robot uses
the world itself as its own representation – continually referring
to its sensors rather than to an internal world model." Looking
back at the Frame Problem, he wrote:

And why could my simulated robot handle it? Because it was
using the world as its own model. It never referred to an internal
description of the world that would quickly get out of date if
anything in the real world moved.

Brooks's approach is an important advance, but Brooks's robots
respond only to *fixed isolable features* of the environment, not
to context or changing significance. Moreover, they do not learn.
They are like ants, and Brooks aptly calls them "animats." But
by operating in a fixed world and responding only to the small
set of possibly relevant features that their receptors can pick up,
Brooks' animats beg the question of changing relevance and so
finesse rather than solve the Frame Problem.

3. What is the proper role of computer science and/or in-
formation theory in relation to other disciplines, including other philosophical areas?

The role of a computer-model based cognitive science ought to be
to show that – as Jerry Fodor says – "the mind doesn't work like
that." As Fodor says:

What our cognitive science has done so far is mostly to throw
some light on how much dark there is. So far, what our cognitive
science has found out about the mind is mostly that we don't
know how it works. (Jerry Fodor, The Mind Doesn't Work That
Way, MIT Press, 2001, p.100.)

Computer Scientists should help all fields studying human beings understand why our everyday coping can't be understood
in terms of inferences from symbolic representations, as Minsky's

intellectualist approach assumed, and also why it can't be understood in terms of responses caused by fixed features of the environment, as in Brooks' empiricist model. AI researchers need to consider the possibility that embodied beings like us take as input energy from the physical universe, and respond in such a way as to open themselves to a world organized in terms of their needs, interests, and bodily capacities without their *minds* needing to impose meaning on a meaningless given, as Minsky's frames require, nor their *brains* converting stimulus input into reflex responses, as in Brooks's animats.

4. What do you consider the most neglected topics and/or contributions in late 20th century studies of computation and/or information?

Our experience of the everyday world is given as already organized in terms of significance and relevance, and that significance can't be constructed by giving meaning to brute facts – both because we don't normally experience brute facts and, even if we did, no value predicate could do the job of giving them situational significance. Yet, all that the organism can receive is mere physical energy. How can such senseless physical stimulation be experienced directly as significant? All generally accepted neuro-models fail to help, even when they talk of dynamic coupling, since they still accept the basic Cartesianmodel, viz:

1. The brain *receives input* from the universe by way of its sense organs (the picture on the retina, the vibrations in the cochlea, the odorant particles in the nasal passages, etc.).

2. Out of this stimulus information, the brain abstracts *features*, which it uses to *construct a representation* of the world.

This is supposedly accomplished either (a) by applying rules such as the frames and scripts of GOFAI (Good Old Fashioned AI); an approach that is generally acknowledged to have failed to solve the Frame Problem. Or (b) by strengthening or weakening weights on connections between simulated neurons in a simulated neural network depending on the success or failure of the net's output as defined by the net designer. Significance is thus added *from outside* since the net is not seeking anything. This approach does not even try to capture the animal's way of actively determining the significance of the stimulus on the basis of its past experience and its current arousal.

Both these approaches treat the computer or brain as a passive receiver of bits of meaningless data, which then have to have significance added to them. The big problem for the traditional neuro-science approach is, then, to understand how the brain binds the relevant features to each other. That is, the problem for normal neuro-science is how to pick out and relate features relevant to each other from among all the independent, isolated features picked up by each of the independent isolated receptors. For example, is the redness that has just been detected relevant to the square or the circle shape also detected in the current input? This problem is the neural version of the Frame Problem in AI: How can the brain keep track of which facts in its representation of the current world are relevant to which other facts? Like the Frame Problem, as long as the mind/brain is thought of as passively receiving meaningless inputs that need to have significance and relevance added to them, the binding problem has remained unsolved and is almost certainly unsolvable. Somehow the phenomenologist's description of how the active organism has direct access to significance must be built into the neuroscientific model.

Fortunately, there is at least one model of how the brain could avoid the binding problem. Walter Freeman, a founding figure in neurodynamics and one of the first to take seriously the idea of the brain as a nonlinear dynamical system, has worked out an account of how the brain of an active animal can directly pick up and augment significance in its world. On the basis of years of work on olfaction, vision, touch, and hearing in alert and moving rabbits, Freeman has developed a model of rabbit learning based on the coupling of the rabbit's brain and the environment.

While all other researchers assume the passive reception of input from the universe, Freeman, like Merleau-Ponty on the phenomenological level, and J.J. Gibson on the (ecological) psychology level, develops a third position between the intellectualist and the empiricist ones. Merleau-Ponty, Gibson, and Freeman take as basic that the brain is embodied in an animal moving in the environment to satisfy its needs.

Freeman maintains that information about the world is not gained by detecting meaningless features and processing these features step-by-step upwards toward a unified representation. The binding problem only arises as an artifact of trying to interpret the output of isolated cells in the receptors of immobilized organisms. Rather, Freeman turns the problem around and asks: Given that the environment is already significant for the animal, how can the animal select a unified significant figure from the noisy background? This turns the binding problem into a selection problem. But this selection is not among patterns existing in the world but among patterns in the animal that have been formed by its prior interaction with the world.

In Freeman's neurodynamic model, the animal's perceptual system is primed by past experience and arousal to seek and be rewarded by relevant experiences. In the case of the rabbit, these could be carrot smells found in the course of seeking and eating a carrot. When the animal succeeds, the connections between those cells in the rabbit's olfactory bulb that were involved are strengthened according to the widely accepted Hebbian rule, which holds that synapses between neurons that fire together become stronger, as long as the synchronous firing is accompanied by a reward. The neurons that fire together wire together to form what Hebb called *cell assemblies*. The cell assemblies that are formed by the rabbit's response to what is significant for it are in effect tuned to select the significant sensory input from the background noise. For example, those cells involved in a previous narrow escape from a fox would be wired together in a cell assembly. Then, in an environment previously experienced as dangerous, those cell assemblies sensitive to the smell of foxes would be primed to respond.

Freeman dramatically describes the brain activity involved:

If the odorant is familiar and the bulb has been primed by arousal, the information spreads like a flash fire through the nerve cell assembly. First, excitatory input to one part of the assembly during a sniff excites the other parts, via the Hebbian synapses. Then those parts reexcite the first, increasing the gain, and so forth, so that the input rapidly ignites an explosion of collective activity throughout the assembly. The activity of the assembly, in turn, guides the entire bulb into a new state by igniting a full-blown burst. (Walter J. Freeman, "The Physiology of Perception," *Scientific American*, Vol. 242, February 1991, p.83.)

Specifically, after each sniff, the rabbit's olfactory bulb goes into one of several possible states that neural modellers traditionally call energy states. A state tends toward minimum "energy" the way a ball tends to roll towards the bottom of a container, no matter where it starts from within the container. Each possible minimal energy state is called an *attractor*. The brain states that tend towards a particular attractor no matter where they start in the basin are called that attractor's *basin of attraction*. As the brain activation is pulled into an attractor, the brain in effect selects the meaningful stimulus from the background.

Thus the stimuli need not be processed into a representation of the current situation on the basis of which the brain then has to infer what is present in the environment. Rather on Freeman's account, the rabbit's brain forms a new basin of attraction for each new significant class of inputs. Freeman contends that each new attractor does not *represent*, say, a carrot, or the smell of carrot, or even what to do with a carrot. Rather, the brain's current state is the result of the sum of the animal's past experiences with carrots. What in the physical input is directly picked up and resonated to when the rabbit sniffs, then, is the affords-eating, and the brain state is directly coupled with (or in Gibson's terms resonates to) the affordance offered by the current carrot.

Freeman has actually programmed his model of the brain as a dynamic physical system, and so claims to have shown what the brain is doing to provide the material substrate for Heidegger's and Merleau-Ponty's phenomenological account of everyday perception and action. This may well be the new paradigm for the Cognitive Sciences.

5. What are the most important open problems concerning computation and/or information and what are the prospects for progress?

There is, however, a big remaining problem. Merleau-Ponty's and Freeman's account of how we directly pick up significance and improve our sensitivity to relevance depends on our responding to what is significant for *us* given our needs, body size, ways of moving, and so forth, not to mention our personal and cultural self-interpretation. If we can't make our brain model responsive to the *significance* in the environment *as it presents itself specifically for human beings*, the project of developing an embedded and embodied model of the mind can't get off the ground.

Thus, to program Heideggerian AI, we would not only need a model of the brain functioning underlying coupled coping such as Freeman's; we would also need – and here's the rub – a model of *our particular way of being embedded and embodied* such that what we experience is significant for us in the particular way that it is. That is, we would have to include in our program a model of a body very much like ours with our needs, desires, pleasures, pains, ways of moving, cultural background, etc.

So, according to the view I have been presenting, even if the Heideggerian/Merleau-Pontian approach to AI suggested by Freeman is ontologically sound in a way that GOFAI was not, a neurodynamic computer model would still have to be given a detailed description of a body and motivations like ours if things were to count as significant for it so that it could learn to act intelligently in *our* world. We have seen that Heidegger, Merleau-Ponty, and Freeman offer us hints of the elaborate and subtle body and brain structures we would have to model and how to model some of them, but this only makes the task of a Heideggerian AI seem all the more difficult and casts doubt on whether we will ever be able to accomplish it.

9

Luciano Floridi

Professor of Philosophy

Research Chair in Philosophy of Information

University of Hertfordshire

Fellow, St Cross College, University of Oxford, UK

There were many reasons why I was initially drawn to informational issues. Let me try to summarise them under four headings.

The first reason was anti-metaphysical. I was drawn to what I later defined as the philosophy of information because, in the late eighties, I was looking for a conceptual framework in which psychologism, introspection, armchair speculations and all those linguistic (or perhaps one should say, Anglo-Saxon, or Indo-European) intuitions could be monitored, tamed and kept under tight control. I shared with Popper a desire for an "epistemology without the knowing subject", as the title of one of his papers declared. The sort of philosophy popular at the time smacked too much of bad metaphysics, a sort of betrayal of the purer and cleaner approach defended by Analytic as well as Neopositivist philosophy, which I admired so much (since then, I have somewhat repented and now I consider myself an ex-analytic philosopher). Since I was interested in epistemology and logic, the move from knowledge to information and from inferential to computational processes was almost natural.

The second reason was related to what I like to describe as *methodological minimalism*. I was looking for a more "impoverished" approach, which could allow me to work on more elementary concepts, less worn down by centuries of speculation, and more easily manageable. It seemed that, if one could have any hope of answering difficult questions about complicated issues concerning knowledge, meaning, the mind, the nature of reality or morality, it made sense to try to tackle them at the lowest and less committed level at which one could possibly work. Informational and computational ideas provided such a minimalist approach. To give a concrete example, my interest in artificial agents was motivated by the classic idea that less is more. This is still not very popular among philosophers, who seem to be too much in love with the human subject, his psychology and idiosyncrasies.

The third reason was a lively interest in timely issues. I could not see myself working on one of the great dead philosophers, spending my life trying to rethink someone else's thoughts. It reminded me of something said by Wittgenstein when complaining about his experience as a tutor in Cambridge. He thought that it was like having his brain sucked. Well, I did not wish to be anyone's intellectual parasite; I had enough problems making sense of what I was trying to think. At the same time, I did not wish to commit myself to some theoretical investigation that would have no bearing or connection with our contemporary world. I was happy to leave the safe and comfortable garden of specialised and irrelevant scholastic philosophy in order to engage with more worldly issues. Philosophy should not talk to itself about itself, and when it does it is utterly sterile. I reasoned that, if the scientific revolution could attract a Descartes, we could definitely engage with the new information revolution, the most radical change that humanity has experienced in history for a long while. I thought this was more than sufficient to justify a robust, philosophical interest in computational and informational issues. It was a risky bet that seems to have paid back handsomely.

The last reason is the simplest: I was born to be a nerd, and what is a nerd without his computer?

It is clearly difficult and somewhat embarrassing to indicate examples from my work, and the work of others, which best illustrates the fruitful use of a computational and/or informational approach for foundational researches and/or applications.

Regarding the work of others, this volume contains contributions from some of the most influential thinkers in the field, more senior colleagues from whom I have learnt much. It would be enough to check their bibliographies to appreciate how deeply and widely the new computational and informational paradigm has influenced our ways of thinking and doing philosophy. As for my own work, this may require a longer answer. If I were to pick up one example, perhaps I would mention the use of Level of Abstractions (LoAs) in conceptual analysis. The idea is simple, powerful, and very common in computer science but its importance and fruitfulness are still not fully appreciated in philosophical circles. Let me summarise it.

The method of LoAs comes from modelling techniques developed in an area of Computer Science, known as *Formal Methods*, in which discrete mathematics is used to specify and analyse the behaviour of information systems. Before I introduce a quick summary of the method of Levels of Abstraction, an everyday example may be useful.

Suppose we wish to describe the state of a traffic light in Rome. We might decide to consider an *observable*, named *colour*, of *type* {*red, amber, green*} that corresponds to the colour indicated by the light. This option abstracts the length of time for which the particular colour has been displayed, the brightness of the light, the height of the traffic light, and so on. So the choice of type corresponds to a decision about how the phenomenon is to be regarded. To specify such a traffic light for the purpose of construction, a more appropriate type might comprise a numerical measure of wavelength. Furthermore, if we are in Oxford, the type of colour would be a little more complex, since – in addition to red, amber and green – red and amber are displayed simultaneously for part of the cycle. So, an appropriate type would be {*red, amber, green, red-amber*}. What we have just seen is a basic concept of *Level of Abstraction*, understood as a finite but non-empty set of observables, where an *observable* is just an *interpreted typed variable*, that is, a typed variable together with a statement of what feature of the system under consideration it stands for.

The definition of observables is only the first step in studying a system at a given LoA. The second step consists in deciding what relationships hold between the observables. This, in turn, requires the introduction of the concept of system "behaviour".

Not all values exhibited by combinations of observables in a LoA may be realised by the system being modelled. For example, if the four traffic lights in Oxford are modelled by four observables, each representing the colour of a light, the lights should not in fact all be green together (assuming they work properly). In other words, the combination in which each observable is green should not be realised in the system being modelled, although the types chosen allow it. Some technique is therefore required to describe those combinations of observable values that are actually acceptable. The most general method is simply to describe all the allowed combinations of values. Such a description is determined by a predicate, whose allowed combinations of values we call the "system behaviours". A *behaviour* of a system, at a given LoA, is defined to consist of a predicate whose free variables are observables at that LoA. The substitutions of values for observables that make the predicate true are called the *system behaviours*.

A *moderated LoA* is defined to consist of a LoA together with a behaviour at that LoA. For example, human height does not take arbitrary rational values, for it is always positive and has an upper limit of (say) nine feet. The variable h, representing height, is therefore constrained to reflect reality by defining its behaviour to consist of the predicate $0 < h < 9$, in which case any value of h in that interval is a "system" behaviour.

Since Newton and Leibniz, the behaviours of the analogue observables have typically been described by differential equations. A small change in one observable results in a small, quantified change in the overall system behaviour. Accordingly, it is the rates at which those continuous observables vary which is most conveniently described. The desired behaviour of the system then consists of the solution of the differential equations. However, this is a special case of a predicate: the predicate holds at just those values satisfying the differential equation. If a complex system is approximated by simpler systems, then the differential calculus provides a method for quantifying the approximation. The use of predicates to demarcate system behaviour is essential in any (nontrivial) analysis of discrete systems because in the latter no such continuity holds: the change of an observable by a single value may result in a radical and arbitrary change in system behaviour. Yet, complexity demands some kind of comprehension of the system in terms of simple approximations. When this is possible, the approximating behaviours are described exactly, by a predicate, at a given LoA, and it is the LoAs that vary, becoming more comprehensive and embracing more detailed behaviours, until the final LoA accounts for the desired behaviours. Thus, the formalism provided by the method of abstraction can be seen as doing for discrete systems what differential calculus has traditionally done for analogue systems.

Specifying the LoA at which one is working means clarifying, from the outset, the range of questions that (a) can be meaningfully asked and (b) are answerable in principle. In standard terminology, the input of a LoA consists of the *system* under analysis, comprising a set of *data*; its output is a *model* of the system comprising *information*. The quantity of information in a model varies with the LoA: a lower LoA, of greater resolution or finer granularity, produces a model that contains more information than a model produced at a higher, or more abstract, LoA. Thus, a given LoA provides a quantified commitment to the kind and amount of information that can be "extracted" from a system. The choice of a LoA pre-determines the type and quantity of data that can be considered and hence the information that can be contained in the model. So, knowing at which LoA the system is being analysed is indispensable, for it means knowing the scope and limits of the model being developed.

Clearly, this is a very powerful and flexible method in any context that requires rigorous conceptual analyses. In philosophy, it should be taught to undergraduates in their first year. It seems the ABC of any decent way of doing philosophy. Unfortunately, too often philosophical difficulties are generated either by a lack of attention for the specific LoA at which the investigation is being developed – as if one could ask questions in a LoA-free environment – or by the wrong choice of the LoA altogether. To give two simple examples: when people ask what a mind is, they often make the first kind mistake; and when they ask whether artificial agents might be moral agents they often make the second kind of mistake. Both could be easily avoided by paying some attention to the method of abstraction.

The proper role of computer science and information science in relation to other disciplines is probably twofold.

On the one hand, computer and information sciences are the new epistemic enablers. They play, indeed they have directly inherited, the role enjoyed by mathematics in the scientific revolution between the seventeenth and the nineteenth century. We all know that there would be no science today without the information/computational turn that took place roughly fifty years ago. This key role played by computer/information sciences will have many fundamental implications. For reasons of space, let me just highlight two of them, one positive and the other negative. Computational-informational approaches and the increasing possibility of *in silico* experiments and simulations will promote crossdisciplinarity and the development of new roles, just think of the new developments in biocomputational research, in neuroscience or in nano-technological engineering. At the same time, we will run a serious risk of disregarding those lines of research that might not easily lend themselves to a computational/informational treatment. Some mis-directed attempts to overuse computers in the Humanities, for example, are a clear sign of this limit and bias. Humanities computing and e-learning projects are well-known for attracting comparatively disproportionate funding compared to more old-fashioned projects of research. Today it is easier to obtain a grant for a database of dubious value than to hire a postdoc for philosophical research. This is where more awareness of the scope and hence of the limits of the informational revolution, in terms of applied research in the humanities, may help us to keep a healthy balance between what is doable and what needs to be done.

On the other hand, as far as philosophy is concerned, it seems that computer and information sciences can, and indeed do, play today the sort of pivotal role that physics and mathematics enjoyed in modern philosophy. If the philosophy of information is becoming our *philosophia prima*, this is also because computational and informational ideas and artefacts are today so essential for our scientific development. So, there can be a twofold relation here. We can take from computer and information sciences many interesting and valuable tools with which to identify, analyse and then seek to solve philosophical problems. And we can use philosophy to explain and make sense of issues arising in computer and information sciences and their applications. It is a symbiotic relation that is already showing excellent results.

One of the most neglected topics in late twentieth century studies of computation and information is a *philosophy of nature* in the widest sense of the word (that is, in the German sense of *Naturphilosophie* as this was used by Shelling and Hegel).[1] Partly because of the predominant debate on AI; partly because, during the twentieth century, the sciences of the physical world became increasingly mathematical and detached from the natural environment, when compared to the situation in the nineteenth century; partly for other reasons too long to explain here (the two cultures, extreme specialization, scholasticisation of the philosophical discourse, etc.), the fact is that, during the last few decades, we have witnessed a growing gap between philosophers of the artificial and philosophers of the natural. The former look exclusively (no matter whether more favourably or critically) on the development of engineered or artificial artefacts, all the way down to the emergence of whole environments. Herbert Simon is a good example. The latter are more likely to be philosophers nostalgic for some utopian state of nature, or a mythical pristine condition of Being.

---

[1] The relevant entry in Wikipedia is reliable: http://en.wikipedia.org/wiki/Naturphilosophie.

Heidegger is notoriously a case in question. The result has been a revival of the old tension between *techne* and *sophia*. This is unfortunate because utterly fruitless. So it will be important to overcome this divide and seek to develop a philosophy of nature that could reconcile the synthetic with the authentic. Bacon and Wiener are two important thinkers in this tradition, whose lessons should be revaluated.

In a recent series of talks and articles, I have argued that the information revolution may be described as the fourth step in the process of dislocation and reassessment of humanity's fundamental nature and role in the universe. We are not immobile, at the centre of the universe (Copernican revolution), we are not unnaturally separate and diverse from the rest of the animal kingdom (Darwinian revolution), and we are very far from being Cartesianminds entirely transparent to ourselves (Freudian revolution). We are now slowly accepting the idea that we might not be dramatically different from other informational entities and agents and smart, engineered artefacts (Turing revolution). In view of this important change in our self-understanding and of the sort of IT-mediated interactions that we will increasingly enjoy with other agents, whether biological or artificial, I suspect that the future challenge will be to develop a philosophy of the Infosphere, where this is understood as synonymous with Being/Nature, which does not privilege the natural or untouched, but treats as authentic and genuine all forms of existence and behaviour, even those based on artificial, synthetic or engineered artefacts. We need to develop a synthetic environmentalism for all entities.

10

Tony Hoare

Principal Researcher

Microsoft Research Ltd.

Cambridge, UK

What? How? Why? and Are you sure?

I would characterise my research activities as basic scientific research into the foundations and principles of computer programming. Together with research colleagues in many countries, we have aimed at the scientific ideal of total correctness of computer programs. We have been driven by scientific curiosity to explore the answers to the basic questions of Science: the What, the Why and the How of the phenomena under investigation. And most important of all, there is the question: How can we be sure that the answers to these previous questions are correct? The greatest possible assurance available to a scientist is that achieved by mathematical calculation or proof. Mathematical proofs can be checked automatically, or even generated by computer. Computer Scientists seek to realise this possibility by getting a computer to check the correctness of its own programs, before even starting to obey them. This check could help to reduce the current costs of error in the all-pervasive computer programs that our society now depends on for our health, our prosperity, and even for our entertainment.

The Problem of Programming Error

I expect that most of you are familiar with the problem of programming error, perhaps even without knowing it. I will tell you the easiest way to recognise the problem. Take almost any of the products that you can buy in a shop, and that you have to switch on before using. It could be a washing machine, refrigerator, a television, a telephone, a personal computer, a game console, a car, or even a bed. Sometimes, for no reason that you can fathom, the device begins to behave in a peculiar way. Perhaps it just fails altogether to respond to your command, no matter how hard or how often you press its buttons. Well, that is very probably due to an error in the programs that have been embedded in your device to control its operation.

Fortunately, the fault can usually be mended very easily. Just switch the device off and switch it on again. Often it starts working again. And now you know for certain that it was an error in the program that caused the fault: there is no point in looking for any other cause.

Programming errors are not like other familiar faults that afflict mechanically engineered products. They are not due to wear and tear; they are not due to rust of metals or to dust in the works. They are due purely to oversights and mistakes that are built into the device by its original designers, long before it even appeared in the shops. What was the mistake precisely? Nobody knows, and nobody ever will. The plain truth is that nobody cares very much.

But sometimes, somebody does care a lot. When the same kind of error occurs in a medical device, intended to deliver a carefully calibrated dosage of radiation, the patient can die. When the same kind of error occurs in a space vehicle (as on the first launch of the European space vehicle Ariane V), the whole mission has to be aborted, at a cost of up to a billion dollars. When the same kind of error occurs on the internet, it makes millions of computers vulnerable to attack by viruses, worms, bots, and other malware. A single successful virus attack, like the infamous Code Red virus, can cost up to two billion dollars to the world economy. And the precautions that are taken against these errors can be just as expensive. The prevention of the millennium bug in the year 2000 was estimated to cost four billion dollars.

But these are just the spectacular tips of a much deeper iceberg. A recent report commissioned by the US Department of Commerce made a survey of the total cost of programming errors, including the cost of detecting them, correcting them, compensating for them, working around them, guarding against them, as well as direct costs of suffering from them. When extrapolated to the entire world economy, the figures gathered in the survey suggest losses of up to one hundred billion dollars per year. Rather more than half of this vast sum falls (in quite small doses) on the millions of users of software products; and the rest falls upon the thousands of engineering companies that produce the software. Is there anything that scientific research can contribute towards a solution of the problem, and the saving of all this money? That is the question that has been addressed by my own research, and that of many research centres.

My Story Starts

My interest in programming errors is attributable to my own personal experience of making mistakes. In my school-days, I studied the classical languages Latin and Greek. Every week my homework included the translation of a paragraph of English prose or verse into one of these languages. It was always an enjoyable challenge to reformulate the original ideas expressed in English into a language whose sentences have a different structure, and whose words have different connotations. But every week, I would make far too many horrible grammatical mistakes. Adjectives in classical languages are supposed to agree with their qualified nouns in three ways: in number, in gender, and in case. In my translations, far too often they didn't.

In 1960, the first job of my career was working for a small computer manufacturer. Because of my linguistic background, I was soon given responsibility for writing a computer program that would translate automatically from one language to another. The source language was a mathematical notation called ALGOL 60, a new language for writing computer programs, similar to those widely used today. The target of the translation was the binary numerical machine code of instructions obeyed by the hardware of the particular computer manufactured and marketed by my employer. Fortunately, both of these languages are artificial languages, very much simpler than English, Latin or Greek. The grammar of ALGOL 60 was so simple that it could be defined by under a hundred mathematical equations, using concepts and notations invented by the great linguistic philosopher Noam Chomsky. Following these rules, my translator could check the grammar of every program submitted to it, and ensure that an ungrammatical program was never passed on for execution by the computer. A mathematically rigorous check of the grammar is an essential first step to ensuring the correctness of a program.

Unfortunately, there are many other kinds of programming error that can be made, even in a grammatically correct program. They are called semantic errors, in contrast to the simpler syntactic errors detected by a language translator. I knew about semantic errors, because they were distressingly frequent in the programs I wrote myself. Would it not be wonderful to have an automatic translator that would check against these kinds of error too? The translator would be based on a set of mathematical equations, like those that defined the grammar; but they would define all the other aspects of the meaning of the programming language. Such a translator was proposed by Bob Floyd in 1967, under the title of a 'Verifying Compiler'. It has since been a holy grail for research into the principles of programming.

In 1968, I moved from industry to the Queen's University in Belfast, to embark on a search for this grail. I realised that the University was the right place for long-term research, whose results were not going to be directly applicable in Industry within some foreseeable timescale. In fact, I predicted that my research would not be applied in practice until after I had reached my academic retirement age, which would be in 1999.

Scientific Curiosity

Because of its long timescales, academic research has to be driven by an ingrained and persistent scientific curiosity to ask the basic questions about the underlying nature of the world. The form of these questions is independent of the choice of a particular branch of Science or its particular subject of study, whether it is animal, vegetable or mineral, whether it is a natural phenomenon in the real world, or an artefact of human engineering. The first question asked by a scientist is 'What does it do?' The next question probes a bit deeper, and asks 'How does it work?' The next question is deeper still, and asks 'Why does it work?' – what are the mathematically expressed laws of nature on which its working relies? Finally, the question on which the scientist expends the greatest effort: 'Are you sure that the answers to these questions are correct?' It is the continuous assembly of more and more convincing evidence that distinguishes science from practical engineering, and all other significant exercises of human intellect.

The first question is: 'What does the program do?' The answer should ideally take the form of an engineering specification of exactly what it is that we *want* the program to do. The language of the specification should have a precise scientific or even mathematical meaning; yet each specification expressed in the language should be so simple and clear, that conformity to the intentions and desires of the user of the program are as obvious as possible. Accurate specification is an essential prerequisite to correct programming, because it defines for each individual program what it means for that program to be correct. In fact, there are flourishing schools of research devoted to dependability engineering, and the elicitation of specifications that encapsulate the true requirements of the user of a program. But all schools of research are agreed on the necessity of a specification which communicates the requirements of the user of a program to the engineer who implements it.

If there is no specification for a program, the only answer to the question 'What does the program do?' is 'Just try it and see!' Such experiments by the user are an enormous waste of time. What is worse, in the absence of specification, there can be no guarantee of the performance of the product, nor any assurance of its fitness to purpose. In fact, it is notorious that software sold today explicitly disclaims all such liability. In other branches of engineering and commerce, such a disclaimer of responsibility would have no legal force.

The second question is 'How does the program work?' As for other objects of scientific study, this question is answered by listing the main components of the program, and describing how they interact with each other across the interfaces that separate them. In other words, the internal interfaces of each component need specification with just as much care as the external interface of the whole program with its user. The language for such internal specifications deals in concepts relevant only inside a computer, and it will be more technical and specialised than the language of external specifications. The internal interface specifications are known as assertions. They are mathematical expressions that are intended to be true at designated places in the execution of the program, when execution passes across an interface between one part of the program and another.

Accurate explanation of how a program works is essential to the design of correct programs. Otherwise the only way to understand the program is by reading the intricate details of its code – many thousands or even millions of interconnected and interacting instructions. This consumes far too much of a programmer's time. Furthermore, it greatly increases the risk of introducing further error when changing the program to improve performance or to meet the evolving needs of its users.

The third question is 'Why does the program work?' The answer is given by the theory of programming. It is this theory which gives meaning to the programs expressed in the relevant programming language. It thereby ensures that a program correctly assembled from correct components will itself give correct results whenever it is executed. If you cannot explain why it is that a program works, it is difficult to plan an implementation project by assigning responsibility for its components among a team of programmers. What is worse, when an error occurs in a program, it is impossible to say which component was responsible for it.

The fourth and final question is 'How do we know that the answers to the previous three questions are correct?' That is the function of the Verifying Compiler, which will be capable of analysing the correspondence between what we want the program to do, and what it actually does. In most branches of science, such checking of the conformity of theory with experiment, or of design with theory, involves possibly lengthy arithmetic calculations with numbers, often based on differential equations and their solution. In most branches of engineering, the routine conduct of essential safety checks is enforced by law. In the case of computer programs, the task of verification is even more complicated; instead of numerical calculation, verification has to exploit the concepts of logical proof. The ideas of logic originated from early researches in Philosophy, dating all the way back to Aristotle and beyond. The techniques of proof were pursued by geometers like Pythagoras and Euclid. Reasoning in modal logic was developed by theologians in the Middle Ages, and applied to exploring concepts such as omniscience, omnipotence, time, and duty. The goal of reducing all logical reasoning to mechanical calculation was first formulated by the German philosopher and polymath Leibniz, who also invented differential calculus. Leibnitz' aspirations were realised in the work of Bertrand Russell, the English philosopher and political activist.

My Story Continues

I first became interested in Philosophy and the foundations of Mathematics when I was still at school. In the afternoons, when my schoolmates were playing cricket or rugby football, I would spend my time in the School Library, reading books of philosophy – Plato, Joad, and especially Bertrand Russell. I was attracted by Russell's crisp and witty writing style. I was interested in his then unconventional views on Marriage and Morals (1929). I read his History of Western Philosophy (1945), and his exploration of Human Knowledge: its Scope and Limits (1948). Finally, his Introduction to Mathematical Philosophy (1919) taught me that the whole of mathematical reasoning is governed by a small collection of simple axioms and rules for the construction of proofs. The basic axioms of arithmetic and calculus and all other branches of mathematics can be derived from axioms stating the basic properties of mathematical sets. The simple rules for proof give the best available justification for our strong conviction that the theorems of mathematics are true.

I moved to Oxford University in 1952 as a classical scholar, continuing my studies of Latin and Greek. I took up residence in Merton College, where I met a group of mathematicians and classicists who shared my interest in mathematical logic. We used to meet late at night, after the pubs were closed, to study the Methods of Logic from a book by Quine (1950). In my final years at Oxford I specialised in Philosophy, both ancient and modern. One of my assignments was to read a famous philosophical article by Alan Turing, about the limits of the capability of his imaginary computer, the Turing Machine. It shares many of its properties with modern computers, including the ability to check the correctness of proofs of mathematical theorems.

It was my study of Russell and Quine and Turing together with my experience of programming and programming language translation that inspired my move in 1968 from an Industrial career to University life at the Queen's University, Belfast. The plan of my research was to express the concepts of computer programming, like the concepts of mathematics, as a collection of mathematical equations, axioms and proof rules that could be used to prove the correctness of computer programs with the same certainty as the proof of mathematical theorems. The first research paper that I wrote as an academic was entitled An Axiomatic Basis for Computer Programming (1969).

Scientific Ideals

When I worked in Industry, I accepted that my first obligation was to the viability and prosperity of the Company that employed me. I discharged this obligation by providing a software support service to customers who bought the Company's computers. It was customer need that set my priorities, which often had to be discharged within a short timescale. The personally expressed satisfaction of the individual customer was a measure of my success.

But when I moved to academic life, my purpose was to become a scientist. Scientists are idealists. They pursue knowledge for its own sake. They pursue with equal dedication the ideals relevant to their branch of science. Thus, physicists pursue the ideal of accuracy of measurement of physical quantities – time, distance, temperature, etc. If current technology is capable of measurement to an accuracy of 99.99 percent, a scientist's goal is to increase this to 99.999 percent; or even further. Chemists similarly pursue the ideal of purity of materials, the chemical elements and compounds with which they work. Scientists are like athletes, seeking to set up a new world record. They want their record to stand for as long as possible, before it is superseded by an even more spectacular achievement—which is when their publications will stop being cited by other scientists.

Scientists pursue their respective ideals to the uttermost achievable limit, far beyond current or even predictable market needs. And an enlightened society pays for them to do so. History gives many examples where new markets open up, and routinely exploit on an industrial scale the levels of accuracy and purity that have hitherto been achieved only in the scientific laboratory. All computers are now built in factories which achieve previously unbelievable levels of purity by filtration of air.

In the case of research into programming theory, the ideal we pursue is that of absolute program correctness. We do not just want to detect errors more efficiently; we want there to be no errors to detect. In theory we know it is possible, because computer programs are almost totally immune to the kind of ageing and loss of function with time that is inevitable in products of other branches of engineering. It should be as impossible to find an error in a delivered program as it is impossible to find a counterexample to a proven mathematical theorem.

And in theory this can be done. The correctness of a computer program can be stated as a mathematical theorem, and proved by all the techniques available to mathematicians. What is more, the proof itself can be checked by the computer, exploiting the research results of great philosophers and logicians of previous centuries, which were obtained in the idealistic pursuit of scientific knowledge, long before computers were even invented.

My Story Continues in Industry

In 1999 I reached the retirement age for UK University employment, and I received an offer of a job as a Senior Researcher at Microsoft Research Laboratory in Cambridge. I welcomed the chance to return to Industry, and to check the accuracy of the prediction that the results of my research would not be applicable in the software industry until after I had retired from academic life. I was wrong. I found that there are many programmers and teams developing Microsoft products using assertions quite liberally in their programs. But in a more important way I was entirely right. Assertions were not being used as I had hoped, to prove correctness in the programs; they were merely used to help in the detection of errors. The assertions were checked not by strict proof, but merely by getting the computer to evaluate their truth while the program was under test. If the evaluation is ever false, this proves that the program went wrong somewhere in the region of the assertion. It is much easier to diagnose and repair an error detected by assertion failure than one detected only when their symptoms become externally manifest. The assertions were usually removed from the program before it was delivered to the customer. I had never expected assertions to be used in this way, merely to help in the detection of some of the errors in a program. That is still a long way from the scientific ideal of program correctness, which guarantees by mathematical proof that there are no errors to detect.

Since I joined Microsoft, the situation has changed dramatically in favour of increasing the level of verification by mathematical proof. The first change was the introduction into programming practice of the program analysis tools (**PREfix** and **PREfast**), which automatically discover simple but appropriate assertions to put in the interfaces of a program, and then use simple mathematics to check whether they could be violated. This has been effective against generic errors like buffer overflow, which were responsible for many of the early vulnerabilities of commodity software. The tools are far from perfect, and a proportion of the warnings are false alarms, which have to be analysed by human inspection. And there are still significant numbers and classes of errors that will be missed.

Both of these deficiencies are being remedied by current research and development, both inside Microsoft and elsewhere. In particular, the most recent analysis tools use more advanced proof techniques to give a high level of assurance that all errors of the most dangerous kinds have been detected. A particular target has been buffer overflows.

At the same time, the technology of computer proof has made

enormous advances. In the last decade, the basic algorithms have improved in speed by a factor of thirty. This is cumulative on a similar factor of increase in the speed of computer hardware. So proof by computer is now a thousand times faster than it was ten years ago. Remember, a factor of a thousand is the same factor that separates the speed of a supersonic aircraft from that of a crawling baby.

Computer hardware design has been the first benefit from this amazing progress. All standard computers in use today have had essential checks performed on the correctness of their hardware designs. The problems of computer software are much more challenging; but there are thousands of scientists working on them throughout the world. There are already at least half a dozen research prototypes of verifying compilers, designed to check the correctness of computer programs before allowing them to be executed. One of them, known as Spec#, is being developed by my colleagues in Microsoft Research in Redmond. Another is ESC / Java, being supported from University College Dublin. Many more specialised programming tools based on verification are being developed by Universities to meet the specific needs of industry, particularly for computers embedded in aircraft, cars, and other critical applications.

Further research is now directed at making the existing tools more suitable for general use by software engineers in Industry. We need to reduce the requirement for the user to understand the basic science that underlies verification technology. We need to reduce the frequency of assistance needed from the human mathematician. The tools need to evolve from their current use – mainly as prototype scientific instruments for the conduct of experiments in program verification. They need to be delivered as an integrated engineering toolset, suitable for use by programmers and software architects in all areas of computer application.

That is a Grand Challenge, similar to Grand Challenges that have made spectacular advances in other branches of science. The advances are achieved by a collaboration of scientists in industries and universities from around the world. Research in Industry will be aimed at serving clients with short-term needs to remove as many errors as possible from programs before their delivery. Longer term research in Universities will pursue to its limits the goal of absolute correctness for computer programs. In the long term, correctness of programs will be assured during the program development process, by use of a development method that has itself been proved sound. Idealistic research in Universities will be the source of new understanding and new ideas to feed continuously into industrial application.

In conclusion, let me look forward to the day when programming error is a problem from the past; when computer programmers make fewer mistakes than engineers in any other profession, and when computer programs are the most reliable components in any of the expanding range of consumer products that you can buy, and have to switch on before you use.

11

John McCarthy

Professor Emeritus of Computer Science
Stanford University, USA

1. Why were you initially drawn to computational and/or informational issues?

In 1948 September I attended the Hixon symposium on cerebral mechanisms in behaviour. One of its themes was the comparison of the brain with computers, the first of which were under construction. This gave me the idea of intelligent computer systems.

2. What example(s) from your work (or the work of others) best illustrates the fruitful use of a computational and/or informational approach for foundational researches and/or applications?

Newell and Simon's information processing psychology revolutionized psychology, destroying behaviourism .

3. What is the proper role of computer science and/or information theory in relation to other disciplines, including other philosophical areas?

Philosophers need to adopt some of the practices of AI and first study simple variants of phenomena like action, knowledge, belief and context rather than only looking for the most general definitions.

4. What do you consider the most neglected topics and/or contributions in late 20th century studies of computation and/or information?

The use of mathematical logic to represent common sense knowledge and reasoning is neglected by logicians and philosophers even though it was a major goal of Leibniz, Boole, and Frege.

5. What are the most important open problems concerning computation and/or information and what are the prospects for progress?

P=? NP and the representation of common sense information and reasoning.

12

John R. Searle

Department of Philosophy

University of California, Berkeley, USA

---

1. Why were you initially drawn to computational and/or informational issues?

I was never drawn to computational or informational issues as such. Rather I was interested in Cognitive Science and I got into debates with people who had what I thought was a mistaken computational conception of the brain and cognition.

I was one of the founding members of the Berkeley cognitive science group in the late 1970s. I thought that cognitive science promised a break from the behaviorism that had dominated American psychology departments throughout a big chunk of the twentieth century. However, while the cognitive scientists of that era avoided the mistake of behaviorism, they often repeated a similar mistake, and that was to suppose that the brain is a digital computer, and the mind is a program or set of programs running in the brain. A common equation from that era was: mind is to brain as program is to hardware.

$$\frac{\text{Mind}}{\text{Brain}} = \frac{\text{Program}}{\text{Hardware}}$$

I baptized this view "Strong Artificial Intelligence" (Strong AI for short) to distinguish it from weak or cautious AI, according to which the computer is a useful tool for studying the mind as it is useful for studying just about any other subject matter.

Strong AI is very easy to refute. Indeed, it can be refuted in a few sentences. Computer programs are defined purely formally or syntactically, in terms of the manipulation of symbols, usually thought of as 0s and 1s. But minds have something more than formal symbols: they actually have mental contents. Therefore, the computer program by itself is not sufficient for, nor constitutive of, a mind. I illustrated this point with the Chinese Room Argument. According to this argument, someone who is not a speaker of Chinese, me for example, could implement a program for answering questions in Chinese but without any understanding at all of either the questions or the answers. I am locked in a room with some boxes of Chinese symbols (the database). I also have a rulebook written in English for manipulating the symbols (the program). People on the outside pass into the room Chinese symbols which, unknown to me, are questions (the input). I follow the computer program and go through the steps that enable me to give back Chinese symbols which, unknown to me, are answers to the questions (the output). I would pass the Turing test for understanding Chinese, but all the same, I would not understand a word of Chinese solely on the basis of implementing the program. Nor would any other element of the system understand Chinese because neither I nor the system has any way to get from the symbols that it is manipulating to the meanings of the symbols. I think the point is quite obvious, but debate about it has continued for over twenty-five years, and it will probably go on.

There are actually much deeper points at issue here, and the question raises them so I will expand on them. The notion of "information" is one of the most confused notions in contemporary cognitive science, and indeed, in contemporary intellectual life. There are at least three different senses of "information" current in cognitive science and other disciplines today: the observer-independent sense, the observer-relative sense, and the technical information theory sense. Let us consider each of these in order. In one sense of "information," the observer-independent or intrinsic sense, I have in my head information about how to get to San Jose. I know the way to San Jose, and my knowledge is not observer-relative, but is observer-independent or intrinsic. I also have a map in front of me that shows the route from Berkeley to San Jose, so the map also contains 'information' about the way to get from Berkeley to San Jose. But in the sense in which I intrinsically have this information, the map only has it in an observer-relative sense. We have designed and printed the map so that it can store, and be used to extract, information. The map does not actually *know* anything. It doesn't have any information in any intrinsic or observer-independent sense. It is only in the observer-relative sense that it has information. We can use it to extract information. Now, exactly the same distinction between the observer-relative and the observer-independent senses of information also needs to be made for the distinction between the observer-relative and the observer-independent senses of information processing, between myself and the computer in front of me. If you ask me how to get to San Jose, I will tell you how, and thus I will process the question and give you an answer which is the result of my intrinsic or observer-independent information processing. But if I type into my computer, using the right program, the question, "How do I get to San Jose?" the computer will print out an answer. But the computer does not know anything. All it does is manipulate symbols, and the sense in which the computer has information or processes information is exactly the same sense in which the map has information or processes information. *It is observer-relative and not intrinsic.*

This distinction, between the observer-relative and the observer-independent senses of information and information processing, is obvious, but you would be surprised how often it is neglected in Cognitive Science research, because many people think that Cognitive Science is a science of "information processing." And of course there is a sense in which that is true. But what we are interested in is the intrinsic sense of information processing in which actual human beings actually go through information processing when they engage in thought processes.

In addition to the observer-independent and the observer-relative sense, there is also a technical sense of "information" in the mathematical subject of "information theory." Information theory is a branch of applied mathematics, and it is very useful in studies of the transmission of signals of various kinds, but once again, these do not involve information in any intrinsic psychological sense. There is a technical definition of "information" in information theory, but it has no direct psychological relevance because satisfying that definition is not sufficient for having intrinsic information. Information theory, I believe, has turned out to be most useful in circuits used in telephones, television, and other forms of data transmission. "Information" in the technical information theoretical sense has rather little significance for Cognitive Science.

Another confusion clouds the issue. There are lots of processes in the brain which are part of the intrinsic information processing but are not themselves intrinsically informational processes. So for example, when I decide to raise my arm, there is a secretion of acetylcholine in the synaptic cleft of the motor neurons that enables the arm to go up. In an observer-relative, or non-intrinsic sense, we can say the system sends information to the synapses that acetylcholine should be secreted. But the sense of information here, like the sense of information in the computer and the map, is entirely observer-relative. The only actual (intrinsic, observer-independent) information is in my conscious and unconscious thought processes.

So, the notion of "information" is something of a mess in Cognitive Science. The notion of computation suffers from a similar ambiguity. If I add two plus two to get four, I am in a literal sense doing an arithmetical computation. I compute the addition function for two numbers. If I type into my pocket calculator "2 + 2" and it prints out "4" it computes the addition function for these numbers, but it does so only in an observer-relative fashion. There is nothing intrinsic to the electronic circuit that makes it computational. We designed it and use it computationally, but there is no intrinsic computation going on in the computer. It is all observer-relative. Computation in this observer-relative sense is not *discovered* in nature, rather it is *imposed* on physical processes such as state transitions in electronic circuits.

The confusion surrounding the notions of computation and information would have been relatively harmless in Cognitive Science, except for the fact that they distracted attention from where it should really have been focused, that is toward the study of actual brain processes which cause and sustain intrinsic information processing such as conscious and unconscious thought processes in the brain. Fortunately, this neglect is now, I believe, a thing of the past, and cognitive science is moving from a computational-based theory of cognition to a cognitive neuroscience paradigm of cognition. I welcome this development.

2. What example(s) from your work (or the work of others) best illustrates the fruitful use of a computational and/or informational approach for foundational researches and/or applications?

The fruitful use of computation that I know of has been mostly in efforts to simulate various cognitive processes. In my own case, various researchers have made useful attempts to program computers so that they would implement my theory of speech acts. I find this very useful because the programmer is faced with the problem that the steps must be stated quite precisely, and this precision is always valuable.

3. What is the proper role of computer science and/or information science in relation to other disciplines?

I think computers play the same role in philosophy and cognitive science that they play in any other discipline. We find it very useful when studying the stomach or studying molecular biology to do computational models, and the computational model is to the real thing in Cognitive Science as it is in the study of the weather or the study of digestion. Nobody thinks that a computational simulation of digestion will actually digest pizza, or that a computational simulation of a rain storm will leave us all wet. On the contrary, these are simulations and hence representations or models of the various processes involved, and it is useful to have such models provided that we do not confuse the model with the real thing. To suppose that a computational simulation of cognition is real cognition is as mistaken as to suppose that a computational simulation of a hurricane is a real hurricane, or a computational simulation of digestion is really digestion.

4. What do you consider the most neglected topics and/or contributions in late 20th century studies of computation and/or information?

I do not know enough about Computer Science and Information Theory as technical academic disciplines to have an intelligent answer to this question. I will confine myself then to those aspects that are relevant to Cognitive Science. The most neglected topics in studies of computation and information that are psychologically real, that is, that are relevant to Cognitive Science, have to do with the question of how the brain actually works as a physical biological system. The brain is above all a biological organ, and it functions on biological principles, like any other biological organ. A computer is a useful tool in studying the brain, as it is a useful tool in studying any organ, but again, to repeat a point I made earlier, it is a mistake to suppose that the computations going on in the brain have any psychological reality. Some of them do. For example, I am now thinking about how to answer these questions, and that is a psychologically real process going on in my brain. Many other processes in my brain can be *described* computationally, but there are no intrinsic thought processes associated with the computations, unless of course a person is actually doing some computing as part of their thought processes. Other forms

of "computation" are computations only in an observer-relative
sense of the concept of "computation."

5. What are the most important open problems concerning computation and/or information and what are the prospects for progress?

There are two sets of questions about computation and information. One has to do with the practical applications and here the
problems are, as always, to get technically better computers, so
they will be able to process information faster and more effectively.
But the real prospects for the study of information processing in
the brain are precisely the brain sciences. I think we are now in a
wonderful period of brain science. Progress has been very fast. I
was on the President's Council for the Decade of the Brain in the
1990s, and though we did not achieve everything that we hoped
to achieve, all the same, enormous progress was made. There has
never been a period in human history when progress in the study
of the brain has been as great as it is now.

As I suggested earlier, we are moving away from a computational Cognitive Science to a cognitive neuroscience. I welcome
this development, and the idea that all we need to understand in
order to understand the brain is to design computer programs that
we suppose are being implemented in the brain will fade away as
an obsolete scientific theory. I think one of the illusions we have
is that there is a useful notion of "information" which can still
be preserved but which is not the intrinsic information of the sort
that I have when I am thinking about how to get to San Jose.
This illusion was aided by the computational Cognitive Science
paradigm, but with the demise of that paradigm, I hope we can
get rid of the confusions surrounding the notions of "information"
and "computation."

13

Aaron Sloman

Honorary Professor of Artificial Intelligence and Cognitive Science
School of Computer Science, The University of Birmingham, UK

1. How did it start?

I shall first give a high level, shallow overview of the answer, and
then a more detailed answer, providing some of the substance.

1.1 High level overview

The move came originally from my concern about spatial reasoning, which I felt was at the core of important kinds of mathematical reasoning and many other kinds of human capability. That was
the subject of my DPhil thesis (Sloman, 1962), which attempted
to defend some of Immanuel Kant's ideas about synthetic necessary truths (Kant, 1781).

My first encounter with computational models, in 1969, resulted
from the arrival of Max Clowes, an AI vision researcher, in the
Experimental Psychology laboratory at Sussex University.[1] Our
discussions (which also included Keith Oatley) convinced me that
in order to understand key features of human spatial reasoning,
and the spatial reasoning used by some animals, we need to adopt
the design stance[2] and understand the various ways in which perceptual systems and other systems that process information can

---

[1] In principle I could have learnt a great deal from my colleague Margaret
Boden, who, by then, had been reading about and writing about AI. But
for some reason we did not talk about that topic until much later, when
I discovered that she already knew about most of the major developments
in computational cognitive science, as revealed in her second book (Boden,
1978), which became one of the leading introductory AI textbooks, especially
for people in other disciplines, because of her outstanding ability to explain
(and criticise) the important developments in an implementation-independent
way, demonstrated also in (Boden, 2006).

[2] As explained here:
http://www.cs.bham.ac.uk/research/projects/cogaff/misc/design-based-
approach.html

work. That understanding is accelerated by attempting to design and build machines that do such things, which provides a much deeper understanding of the design options and the tradeoffs between them than philosophers can get from arm-chair discussion and speculation.

It soon became clear to me that vision could not be understood in isolation: visual mechanisms work in combination with many others within a complete functioning *architecture*. For example, my interest in vision was originally triggered by its role in mathematical reasoning. Moreover, it was clear that vision not only provided factual information about the environment but also had aesthetic functions, attention control functions, action-control functions, sexual functions, and a variety of different sorts of communication functions, including reading facial expressions and gestures, reading text, reading diagrams, and reading music. So early on I began to think about integrated information-processing architectures combining many different sorts of components, and that eventually led me to the design-based analysis of many other aspects of human minds and animal minds, constantly driven, by the question: what sort of machine could do *that*?

Some of the ideas, including the importance of information processing *architectures* were reported in my 1978 book (written at the behest of Margaret Boden), in which I tried to show (in chapter 2) how the enterprise, like theoretical linguistics, required a broadening of popular conceptions of the nature of science, as well as showing in other sections how it changed our ideas about the nature of mind and relations between mind and body.

The more I learnt, the more I realised how hard the problems were, and how impressive the achievements of evolution were. There are still many unsolved problems requiring interdisciplinary cooperation, and when I can find philosophers, psychologists, neuroscientists, biologists, roboticists, linguists, computer scientists, etc. interested in addressing the issues, I try to learn from and work with them, though they are rare, partly because our educational and research funding systems produce and reward specialists with narrow vision, and also because the educational opportunities promised three decades ago by the development of computing, namely making it possible for many more people to learn how to think about complex working systems were not taken up. The failure, which is one of the great missed opportunities of recent decades, is discussed further in Section 1.2.5.

1.2 A longer version of the story

1.2.1 DPhil Research

My Oxford DPhil thesis in 1962 (now online) was about why Kant was right about mathematical discovery and Hume (and most contemporary analytic philosophers) were wrong. I tried to show why some kinds of mathematical discovery were both substantive (synthetic, in Kant's terminology) and non-empirical (i.e. a priori), for example geometric theorems, originally proved using the human ability to visualise geometric constructions and their consequences.

I kept on thinking about the problems after finishing the DPhil. For example, in Sloman (1965b) I tried to explain some of the distinctions required for understanding Kant's view (e.g. the necessary/contingent, a priori/empirical and analytic/synthetic distinctions) and in Sloman (1965a) extended some of Frege's ideas about functions in an attempt to analyse some sources of necessity. I returned to examining the notion of seeing that something had to be true in Sloman (1968/9.), but I was not really happy with what I was able to say about our ability to "see" necessary structural relationships. Later I realised that I needed new conceptual tools, which AI seemed to be developing.

1.2.2 Meeting Max Clowes

Around 1969 I met Max Clowes, a well known highly charismatic AI vision researcher (Sloman, 1984), who had joined the Experimental Psychology department. Max and I had many discussions and I attended the lectures on programming and AI that he presented to psychology students. The work he and others were doing on interpreting images, used only logical formulae (or equivalent symbolic structures) to express the interpretations. This did not address requirements to keep the interpretation in registration with image features, so that the information produced could be described as "visual" and could be operated on by using its spatial structure. I told him I thought that could be done by adding symbolic information to the image structures. This would also facilitate geometric modes of reasoning about the scenes, which I was sure were needed for many purposes besides visual perception, including geometric reasoning in mathematics.

In 1971, when Max was one of the organisers of the 2nd International Joint Conference on AI at Imperial College London, he persuaded me to submit a paper on my ideas about geometrical reasoning, so I wrote Sloman (1971), attacking the logicist method-

ology propounded by McCarthy and Hayes (1969), which Max
had drawn to my attention. I made a distinction between Fregean
and analogical representations, focusing mainly on their role in
reasoning. This was in part an attempt to clarify the frequently
made distinction between symbolic and pictorial or imagistic representations, often based on the mistaken view that pictures and
diagrams are isomorphic with what they represent, clearly refuted
by 2-D pictures of 3-D objects. Another closely related common
mistake was to think the distinction was about the difference between discrete (or digital) and continuous information structures.
Likewise, most people were unaware of the important features of
symbolic representations that had been analysed by Frege, namely
that they produced more complex structures from simpler ones by
(recursively) applying functions of various sorts to arguments of
various sorts, and making use of compositional semantics. (Sloman, 1965a was an attempt to generalise some of Frege's ideas).

My paper argued that the relationship between an analogical
representation and what it represents is far more subtle than most
people had realised, and, as I had learnt from the work of Clowes
and others, can involve highly context-sensitive modes of interpretation that vary from one part of an image to another, for instance
in a 2-D picture showing several surfaces with different 3-D orien-
tations. The paper also pointed out that reasoning by modifying
a spatial structure (changing either geometric or topological features) had much in common with reasoning by modifying logical
or algebraic formulae, though the latter is much easier to implement on a computer.

I realised then that if we could build a working model of a
human-like visual system we might be able to use it as the basis for a working model of human geometric reasoning in both
mathematics and in every day life (e.g. causal reasoning), making a major contribution both to philosophy of mathematics and
possibly also mathematics education, though I did not have the
programming experience required for that.

1.2.3 A formative year in Edinburgh

Fortunately, after reading my 1971 paper, Bernard Meltzer, head
of the Computational Logic department in Edinburgh University,
and founding editor of the journal *Artificial Intelligence*, in which
he published the paper, obtained a grant from the UK Science
research council to bring me to Edinburgh for a year in 1972-
3. Because there were so many outstanding AI researchers either
based in Edinburgh or visiting during the year, that was an amaz-

ingly educative year for me. Among other things, it was the year in which the Edinburgh AI team got their robot Freddy to assemble a simple toy car and a toy boat, using 3-D vision and a robot hand, a very impressive achievement that has largely been ignored by recent robotic researchers.[3] It was while in Edinburgh that I first learnt about the importance of virtual machines, partly as a result of reading Wegner (1968), and partly as a result of experiencing the benefits of operating systems with virtual memory mechanisms. The Edinburgh POP-2 system on which I wrote my first programs supported up to 8 simultaneous users and allocated each user a virtual address space, which was frequently re-mapped onto the underlying hardware by the garbage collector, in order to optimise use of the very scarce physical memory in the computer (128 Kbytes!). This made it obvious that facts about supervenience in computer virtual machines contradicted widely held philosophical assumptions about supervenience.

1.2.4 Working on vision at Sussex and Birmingham

Soon after returning to Sussex I managed to get my own research council grant for three years, during which I had David Owen and later Geoffrey Hinton as research fellows on a project to test some ideas about the architecture of a human-like vision system. Some of the results of that work are reported in the chapter on vision in (Sloman, 1978a), describing the Popeye vision system which demonstrated how a mixture of concurrent top-down, bottom-up and middle-out processing at different ontological levels could enable rather complex and noisy images to be interpreted, using both the data in the images and prior knowledge about possible contents of the world. This combination of concurrent collaborative computation and prior knowledge explained both the speed of recognition in easy cases and graceful degradation as images grew more complex, features that are often thought to be impossible for systems implemented on computers.

However it was then clear that we were nowhere near a full vision system, and as I continued working on requirements for designing a working vision system over many years[4], I constantly felt that the problems of explaining human vision were far more com-

---

[3] See http://www.aiai.ed.ac.uk/project/freddy/

[4] See Sloman, 1982, 1989, 1994, 1993, 1995, 1996, 1998, 2002b, 2001, 2006.
A very recent example is a discussion paper on predicting affordance changes using spatial reasoning:
http://www.cs.bham.ac.uk/research/projects/cosy/papers/#dp0702

plex and varied than most vision researchers in AI, psychology or neuroscience (with the possible exception of Trehub (1991)) had realised, partly because of the multiplicity of forms of representation involved, and the multiplicity of ontologies involved in perceiving structures and processes in the 3-D environment, and partly because of multiplicity of types of process that could occur in a visual system, e.g. seeing spatial features, spatial structures, spatial structural relations, causal relations, affordances, processes, gestures, facial expressions, social interactions and, as a result of various kinds of learning processes, being able to read written languages, sightread music, read mathematical and programming notations, and reason about mathematical problems. (That is nowhere near a complete list. In particular it omits all the aesthetic functions of vision.)

As pointed out in Sloman (1982), some of these visual abilities involved acquiring and using *transiently available* information about continuously varying processes, information that was lost immediately after use, whereas other visual abilities involved acquiring and storing (at least for a while) *re-usable* information about objects, surfaces, relationships, and constraints that could play a role in reasoning (including planning actions and predicting what was going to happen in the environment) and in communicating information about the environment to others. For instance, in continuous visual control of actions, such as running a finger along a curved line, much transient information is used in making continuous adjustments to the motion, information that is lost after it has been used, unless the information processing architecture allows such processes to be explicitly monitored and information about what they do recorded so that it is available for future use, for instance in future deliberative reasoning. This requires the information to be discretised into categories useful for forming generalisations.[5] This goes beyond the functionality required for performing the actions, though it can support learning that improves how actions are performed. Incomplete understanding of the different ways in which information can be acquired, represented and used in different parts of a multi-functional architecture has led to much confusion among researchers about dual (dorsal and ventral) visual streams and so-called "mirror neurons". If more people

---

[5] Some of the requirements are discussed in more detail in this discussion of "fully deliberative" architectures: http://www.cs.bham.ac.uk/research/projects/cosy/papers/#dp0604

tried to design working models inappropriate theories might not survive so long.

1.2.5 Growing COGS at Sussex

I feel it is necessary to include a section on our work on teaching, because a great deal of what I learnt in the 1970s and 1980s about computing and AI and their relevance to other disciplines, arose from the intense collaboration with colleagues at Sussex in developing new teaching ideas and tools to support the learning. These tools and the related philosophy were, for a while, used in a number of other university departments, and in one UK school (Marlborough College). They also formed the basis of the new AI half degree introduced in Birmingham after I moved there.

After my return to Sussex, a team of colleagues, including Margaret Boden, Max Clowes, then later Steve Hardy, Gerald Gazdar and others, started an undergraduate programme in the Arts and Social Sciences area of the University, in which we taught AI alongside philosophy, linguistics, psychology, and at first anthropology, though that was later dropped as none of the local anthropologists was doing research in the area of overlap. The teaching was highly collaborative and was closely related to our research. A few years later we introduced an undergraduate AI major and also a 'conversion' MSc degree in 'Knowledge Based Systems'. Eventually, this combined activity – undergraduate teaching, MSc teaching, PhD supervision, and research – grew into COGS, The School of Cognitive and Computing Sciences, with Margaret Boden as first Dean. Those were exciting times, with much wide-ranging discussion which helped to extend my ideas though I can't recall details of what I learnt from whom: leading figures with a shared belief that AI could be the glue that held several disciplines together included Max Clowes, Margaret Boden, Steve Hardy, Gerald Gazdar, Chris Mellish, Jonathan Cunningham, and later on David Hogg and David Young, with Steve Isard helping from his base in the Experimental Psychology group, where he taught AI and shared in the development of our teaching materials. Christopher Longuet-Higgins was also there but had only research commitments. We had a stream of distinguished visiting researchers. Alan Mackworth, whose D.Phil was supervised by Max Clowes also contributed in the early years.

Initially we taught AI by using Algol-68 in batch mode on the university central mainframe computer. Frank O'Gorman who then worked for Max Clowes taught me an enormous amount about Algol-68, a sophisticated language that stretched many of my ideas about computation, but was unsuitable for beginner AI students. So we tried using a batch mode version of Pop-2. But it soon became clear that for AI students development and testing had to be interactive: one could not simply develop (or read up) a theory, work out its mathematical formulation, then type in the code with some test input, as some researchers in other disciplines were accustomed to doing. Testing and debugging game playing, or language understanding, or incremental learning programs, needed to be highly interactive. Fortunately, from around 1975 the university gave us funds to buy our own PDP11 computer. We decided that none of the existing readily available AI systems for that machine would meet our needs, so Steve Hardy developed an implementation of the Edinburgh AI programming language POP-2, which he called Pop-11. Although he was the programming expert, several of us were involved in designing features of the language, including Max Clowes and Steve Isard. As a result, Pop-11 extended Pop-2 in several ways, mainly to support AI teaching for students whose background was not necessarily scientific or mathematical. Some of those extensions also made the language more useful for our research, especially the inclusion of a pattern matcher as part of the language.

Contributing to the design and implementation of Pop-11 and its suite of teaching libraries for AI, helped me acquire a much deeper understanding of the nature of computation than I could have had merely as a user of a programming language. This work continued during the 1980s as Pop-11 grew into Poplog, a multi-language development environment with a number of novel features, mostly designed and implemented by John Gibson, who became the chief architect. When it turned out that people in industry wanted to use it we were able to get funds from sales and research grants to help with the development, and eventually Poplog became a successful product, which helped many UK researchers in academe and industry learn about and use AI programming techniques.

Partly because of my own learning experiences, and partly on the basis of our teaching experiences from 1976 onwards, I became convinced that the teaching of programming, and especially teaching children to design, implement, test, debug, document, analyse and compare AI programs, would have a profound effect on the development of education and could lead to important changes in the ways humans understood and thought about structures and processes, including mental structures and processes. Some of those educational ideas were presented in Sloman (1978a) and since then I have tried to document them in online web sites.[6] Unfortunately, this potential was never realised because politicians, educators, teachers and well-meaning parents made the deep mistake of thinking that the most important thing to teach children about computing was how to use the tools they were likely to have to use in their jobs, e.g. word processors, databases, and later web-browsers, etc., instead of how to design, implement, debug, analyse and compare working systems. I often wonder how many politicians who waste tax-payer's money on unworkable schemes (like the UK's national identity card scheme, and the National Health Service IT project[7] might have been more cautious if they had had real experience of trying to make moderately complex systems work.

This enormous missed educational opportunity has mostly gone unremarked (though its consequences are often lamented, without the causes being recognized). Recently, an influential computer scientist (Wing, 2006) has noticed the problem, and has been eloquently recommending a change of direction, but it may now be too late to undo the damage.

The experience of managing the Poplog development team and interacting with the commercial distributors (initially SDL in 1983, and later a start-up company ISL, formed in 1989 by a subset of the main company) also taught me a great deal about AI and its applications. That process continued until I moved to the School of Computer Science at the University of Birmingham in 1991, though I never concealed the fact that I was primarily a philosopher not a computer scientist.

1.2.6 Working on robotics at Birmingham

My ideas about architectures, and especially the relationships between architectures and affective states and processes continued to develop in Birmingham, at first in collaboration with Glyn Humphreys in psychology. I was very lucky to have some excellent PhD students who stretched my mind. For example, Luc Beaudoin, who was investigating architectural requirements for emo-

---

[6] E.g. in these two: http://www.cs.bham.ac.uk/research/projects/ cogaff/misc/compedu.html

http://www.cs.bham.ac.uk/research/projects/ cogaff/misc/dscedu.html

[7] Whose folly is explained here: http://www.cs.bham.ac.uk/research/ projects/cogaff/misc/isoft/

tions, made me realise that the ideas about concurrency in chapter 6 of Sloman (1978a) had to be extended by decomposing some of the higher level processes into concurrent management (e.g. deliberation and problem solving) and meta-management (i.e. monitoring and modifying the management processes, and others), and who also made me realise that a typical decision-tree is not suitable for such meta-management processes, because too many of the sub-problems are interdependent and can interact in ways that an algorithm designer could not anticipate. I have not yet seen any proposed architecture that deals with all the requirements.

For a while my research on vision took a back seat, though I made a number of unsuccessful attempts to get funding for a project to work on a real or simulated robot to explore the relationships between 3-D vision and action, among other things.

My work on those topics progressed slowly, but eventually accelerated as a result of working in a collaborative EU-funded robotic project (http://www.cs.bham.ac.uk/research/projects/cosy/ which started in 2004). Detailed work on requirements for the architecture and representations used by a human-like robot performing everyday domestic tasks, led both to the realisation that perceptual contents are primarily about processes of many sorts (i.e. perceived structures in the environment are really perceived processes with little change) and that understanding vision and understanding causation in the physical environment were closely related. This work accelerated as a result of the arrival in Birmingham of Jackie Chappell, who studies animal cognition, especially bird cognition, in the School of Biosciences. One example of our collaboration is a linked pair of workshop presentations on understanding Humean and Kantian causation.[8] We have also begun to develop new theories about tradeoffs between evolution of cognition and development of cognition (e.g. in Sloman & Chappell, 2005, and Chappell & Sloman, 2007).

Most of the problems are still unsolved: we do not have working visual systems remotely like those of birds or mammals in their capabilities, and a deep model of human spatial understanding and reasoning still seems a long way off (though simple fragments have been modelled in connection with mathematical reasoning in Jamnik, Bundy, and Green (1999) and Winterstein (2005)). We also still lack a philosophical theory of causation, rich enough to be the basis of an implementation of a machine able to engage in

---

[8] http://www.cs.bham.ac.uk/research/projects/cogaff/talks/wonac

Kantian causal reasoning, though there is progress in essentially Humean causal reasoning, based on Bayesian reasoning. We also lack a theory of human learning, though there are many fragments available from many disciplines, most of them still ignored in AI, especially lessons from biology. There has, of course, been a very influential fashion for exploring and attempting replicate biological mechanisms. The mistake is to ignore what the mechanisms are required for. This leads to over-simplified tasks and benchmarks for testing the models.

1.2.7 Evolution, development and GLs

Many people think that to explain human intelligence we must show how an animal or robot with no prior knowledge about the environment, or itself, could use a very general learning capability (such as reinforcement learning), possibly aided by teachers, to acquire all the knowledge it will ever need. This idea has been implausible as regards humans for many decades, and, as McCarthy remarked, "Evolution solved a different problem than that of starting a baby with no a priori assumptions" (McCarthy, 1996).

Many years ago when I learnt that many animals, members of so-called 'precocial' species, show extraordinary competences soon after birth, or hatching, such as young grazing mammals that get up and walk to the mother's nipple, deer that run with the herd, chicks that feed themselves and follow the nearest hen they see after hatching, and many more, I took that as evidence that evolution is capable of producing extremely sophisticated and knowledgeable neonates (apparently with much richer innate knowledge than either Descartes or Kant ever assumed possible).

However, that raised the question: Why do some species, whose adults seem to be particularly intelligent, including nest-building birds, hunting mammals, and primates, especially humans, apparently start off at a much less knowledgeable level? This led to a hunch that the starting point for such 'altricial' animals was actually more sophisticated than it appeared to be, and included mechanisms tailored to our environment in a generic manner, which provided potential for more advanced development than the other species that appeared more intelligent at birth. Ever since then I have been trying to characterise that difference in information processing terms. The work gained a new impetus when Jackie Chappell joined in, as explained above. We have several papers developing ideas about the precocial-altricial (or in our preferred terminology, preconfigured-metaconfigured) spectrum for types of competence, including partial specifications for bootstrapping mechanisms capable of rapidly exploring and learning about the environment on the basis of innate meta-knowledge about what sorts of things can be learnt and how they can be learnt, as opposed to specific knowledge such as precocial species display. Figure 1 summarises some of the ideas we have been developing about routes from the genome to behaviours.

Recently we have argued (reviving some themes from Sloman, 1978b and Sloman, 1979) that the kinds of learning and kinds of competence shown by many animals that lack the ability to communicate in a language with a rich syntax would be impossible if they did not use a type of 'Generalised Language' (GL) *internally* for expressing information that can be complex, highly structured, and very variable. Similar comments apply to pre-linguistic children. More specifically, such languages must support expression of information contents that vary in structure and complexity (unlike the fixed size vectors typical of inputs and outputs of many neural net models) and which support context sensitive compositional semantics. This internal generalised language need not be restricted to combinations of discrete atomic symbols, and may in some cases include geometrical structures used to express meaning and inferences (as emphasised in the 1971 paper).

We conjecture that sophisticated GLs evolved before human language, and are used by some non-human animals, and that young children use complex GLs for internal information processing long before they can use an external language to converse in. This has implications for both the evolution and the development of human language, on which we have a very brief published paper (Sloman & Chappell, 2007) and an online presentation.[9] Some conjectured mechanisms that may be involved in linguistic and other forms of cognitive development, including development of several layers of ontology while learning about the environment, are sketched at a high level of abstraction in (Chappell & Sloman, 2007). There is still much to be done to develop the ideas, and we are hoping that experiments in robotics as well as further research on animal cognition and human learning will shed light on the mechanisms and processes involved. The kinds of innate competence implied by such theories must have many implications for biological as well as robotic research. A good source of information about some of the facts that such mechanisms need to be able to explain is Gibson and Pick (2000). Adequate working models

---

[9]http://www.cs.bham.ac.uk/research/projects/cogaff/talks/#glang

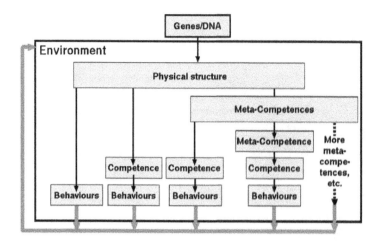

FIGURE 13.1. (Diagram from Chappell and Sloman (2007), produced with help from Chris Miall). This illustrates multiple routes from the genome to behaviours. The routes to the left of the diagram are mostly genetically determined, but the behaviours they produce and the environment's responses combine with genetically determined and acquired meta-competences to produce new competences (including ontology extensions) which generate routes to behaviour further to the right of the diagram. This cognitive epigenetic process includes growth of an information processing architecture which is the joint product of the genome and, at different levels of abstraction, the environment.

could shed new light on Kant's theories about synthetic *a priori* knowledge, in part by explaining how mathematical competences develop.

1.2.8 The central importance of architectures

At a fairly early stage it became clear to me that trying to understand vision on its own was impossible. Likewise other kinds of mental function. In humans and many other animals mental capabilities form a complex integrated system with many components coexisting and interacting concurrently with one another and, in some cases with the environment. This led me to argue that we need to think not just in terms of algorithms and representations, as was then commonplace in AI, but in terms of *architectures*. I wrote a paper on this during my stay in Edinburgh in 1972–3 and it became a departmental discussion paper (Memo 59 Department of Computational Logic, slightly revised and published in 1973 in the AISB Newsletter. A still later version became chapter 6 of

Sloman (1978a).

It also became clear that the notion of architecture was also very important for philosophy. That is because philosophers mostly attempt to analyse concepts related to human mental competences, such as belief, desire, emotion, imagination, learning, memory, creativity, and consciousness, as if these concepts all had clear meanings and "correct" definitions.

However, there are three important facts that impinge on this:

- different animals have different information processing architectures, and humans have different architectures at different stages of development or in some cases because of brain damage or disease;

- different architectures make different sorts of states and processes possible;

- concepts of mind refer to states and processes in complex information processing systems.

It follows that not all mental concepts are applicable to all architectures. This means that instead of philosophers attempting to produce unique and correct analyses for concepts of the sort illustrated above, they should map out ways in which those concepts can be related to different architectures, including allowing that some architectures make certain concepts totally inapplicable.

For example, if a system has a collection of programs that can be triggered into action by different sensor inputs, and if when each program runs nothing else is happening, then that system is incapable of monitoring what it is doing or deciding to modulate what it is doing. So it cannot be described as self aware or self controlled.[10] For philosophers to explore the space of possible architectures and the different families of concepts that are applicable to different sorts of architectures they need to learn to think like designers.

1.2.9 Thinking like a designer about emotions and other forms of affect

Some of the ideas about architectures underpinning various kinds of mental states and processes were further developed after I

---

[10] For more on this see this discussion of logical topography and logical geography: http://www.cs.bham.ac.uk/research/projects/cogaff/misc/logical-geography.html

moved to Birmingham in 1991, and worked with a series of PhD students, initially in collaboration with the psychologist Glyn Humphreys, on trying to clarify notions like, desire, motive, intention, preference, emotion, mood, attention, by showing how they could relate to processes that occur and dispositions that arise in an architecture that we conjectured was typical of a normal adult human being. In particular, Luc Beaudoin, Ian Wright and I tried to show how many of the phenomena of long term emotions, such as grief, jealousy, infatuation, obsessive ambition, and others, which can endure even when they are not being manifested or experienced, though they may easily be triggered into expressing themselves, could be accounted for within the type of architecture we were developing, as reported at length in Wright, Sloman, and Beaudoin (1996).

We proposed an explanation of some of the variety of types of emotion, including enduring but sometimes dormant emotions, by showing how different sorts of emotions (primary, secondary and tertiary, to a first approximation) could arise from the functioning of different architectural layers in one individual, e.g. the evolutionarily oldest reactive mechanisms, newer deliberative mechanisms able to contemplate non-existent but possible states and processes, and meta-management mechanisms that monitor and control other internal processes. This is an oversimplification, but is mentioned as an illustration of the way in which conceptual analysis can be enriched if it is informed by theories about information processing architectures. Our theory contradicts many of the popular views of emotions, e.g. theories treating emotions as involving bodily episodes and experienced mental episodes.

The ideas were further extended in collaboration with Brian Logan, then Matthias Scheutz and Ron Chrisley, e.g. in Sloman, Chrisley, and Scheutz (2005). In contrast with these ideas, the vast majority of emotion researchers interested in computational models seem to treat emotions as definitionally linked to expressive behaviours, and actual mental episodes, rather than enduring but possibly dormant dispositions to produce such behaviours and episodes. I think it will eventually become clear, partly as a result of more sophisticated architecture-based analysis, that current work on affective states and processes focuses on only a tiny subset of the actual variety. Novelists, playwrights and poets are far more comprehensive in their grasp of the phenomena.

2. Examples

Question 2: What example(s) from your work (or the work of others) best illustrates the fruitful use of a computational and/or informational approach for foundational researches and/or applications?

It all depends on what 'fruitful' is supposed to mean. Not everyone will agree on what should be called fruitful. More importantly, it depends on what 'computational' and 'informational' are taken to mean. Neither of those has a clear and generally agreed meaning. As far as I am concerned what is fruitful is the approach that centres on the study of kinds of mechanisms that could explain how systems work, and how processes occur: the design-based approach. The processes in question may include physical and chemical processes, but are dominated by information processing mechanisms, including probably kinds of mechanisms that we have not yet thought of.

2.1 My own work

Anyhow, almost all of my work since about 1971 has been based on the design stance, as illustrated above.

Answering Question 2 would amount to reproducing most of the contents of my online account of topics I have worked on http://www.cs.bham.ac.uk/~axs/my-doings.html.

2.2 Work of others

Almost everything written by John McCarthy and Marvin Minsky, and most of Margaret Boden's work also illustrates this. Also much of the work by Herbert Simon and Allen Newell. A lot of the work by Andy Clark is relevant though as far as I know he has not engaged in developing designs for working systems: rather he works mainly at a methodological level. There are many more, of course, too many to list. In earlier times, even work by Immanuel Kant, Gottlob Frege, Jean Piaget, and Kenneth Craik, among others, was relevant, among others, though they lacked the conceptual tools we now have for thinking about information processing systems, just as we now lack conceptual tools that will be developed in years to come.

3. The proper role?

Question 3: What is the proper role of computer science and/or information theory in relation to other disciplines, including other philosophical areas?

I would not use the phrase "proper role". I would say that there are a number of things about the science of information that are relevant to all aspects of science and philosophy. So people learning in detail about types of information processing systems may gain the following benefits.

The most important single fact is that whereas much philosophical discussion has been about necessary or sufficient conditions for something to be the case, a great deal of such discussion has simply ignored the problem of explaining how processes can occur, and in particular explaining how mental mechanisms work: Above all else, minds do things, even if much of what they do is internal.

Many people know that life cannot be understood if we ignore how its many forms evolved, how individual living things develop, how individuals interact with their environment, including other similar individuals. People simply take it for granted that life is about processes. But they fail to notice that minds do things, and that something that is always static and simply has information (e.g. beliefs, memories, concepts) and states that use information (e.g. desires, preferences, hopes, fears, intentions, etc.), without ever acquiring, manipulating, deriving, constructing and using information, could not be a mind. That means that understanding what minds are requires understanding how all those processes can happen. Unfortunately, when philosophers do try to discuss mechanisms that might explain such processes they often produce vague, incomplete, totally inadequate descriptions because they have no experience of the difference between using a specification to make something that works, and merely talking about such things: learning how to design, test, debug, analyse, compare and criticise working systems is not yet a standard part of the philosophical curriculum, though some of us attempted to produce a new breed of philosophy graduates educated in such matters at the University of Sussex, starting in the mid 1970s.

So the first benefit is learning how to produce explanations of working systems (e.g. minds), in particular explanations that are capable of being tested in working implementations, as opposed to merely looking plausible to readers. This requires learning new ways to think about process and structure, i.e. how structures can produce and constrain processes and how processes can manipulate structures – especially in structures in information processing systems.

Another benefit is learning how to detect inadequate explanations of mental and biological phenomena, e.g. explanations that could not be used as the basis for designing or building a system of the kind whose abilities are being explained.

Understanding the variety of types of virtual machine and the variety of ways in which virtual machines can be implemented or realised in physical machines or other virtual machines, will, I suspect, provide much matter for philosophical analysis in future years.

Those are some of the broad themes associated with learning about computer science, software engineering and the theory of information. More specific benefits include:

Learning how to analyse designs for various kinds of virtual machine as a way of clarifying old philosophical questions, e.g. about types of freedom, the nature of mental states and processes, varieties of consciousness, etc.

Understanding the deep implications of the differences between matter-manipulating, energy-manipulating and information manipulating machines, and their relationships. E.g. information manipulating machines have to be implemented in energy manipulating machines. Matter and energy are conserved (or, to be more precise, mass-energy is conserved) and they are measurable. In contrast information is not conserved: I can give you much of my information without losing any of it. Moreover what is important about information is not usually a measurable quantity but its *content*, i.e. what is referred to, and what properties, relationships, generalisations, are expressed.

Understanding the variety of *requirements* for machines (natural or artificial) with different combinations of information processing competence produced by evolution, e.g. machines like microbes, like insects, like fishes, like reptiles, like birds, like mammals, of many kinds. This includes understanding the information processing demands imposed both by different sorts of environments and by different sorts of physical designs for the animal or machine, as explained in Sloman (2007).

Understanding issues related to (decidability) solvability and complexity which are relevant to the differences between different mechanisms for doing the same task, and to differences between different tasks.

Understanding the role of Turing machines and von Neumann machines within the larger space of possible information processing machines, including the chemical information processing machines used throughout living systems, and machines that grow their architectures.

It must be emphasised that not everyone who studies computing, software engineering or AI and who learns to write computer programs ends up understanding all the above issues. For example, there are now many AI researchers who, because of recent swings of fashion in the field, have no first-hand experience of designing any of the kinds of systems developed in symbolic AI, including systems that manipulate symbolic structures. As a result they know only about neural nets and mechanisms for operating on numbers, matrices, probability distributions and the like, especially mechanisms and processes that are closely coupled with sensori-motor systems. That is a good way to think about most information processing in insects and other invertebrates, but completely ignores many of the interesting competences of birds, humans, and other mammals, including mathematical and philosophical competences of humans.

This leads to a very serious narrowing of vision regarding possible designs and the requirements to which they are suited. This restricted (and often prejudiced) understanding of information processing systems can be found in researchers in several disciplines. I expect the publication of Boden (2006) will help to counter this narrowness, though it will take time.

4. Neglected topics

Question 4: What do you consider the most neglected topics and/or contributions in late 20th century studies of computation and/or information?

I have partially answered this above, e.g. in the last section. More generally, there are two sorts of tasks that have not been properly understood or pursued, with a resulting serious impact in our understanding of natural and artificial information-processing systems, namely:

1. Understanding the variety of designs produced by evolution, including designs that make significant use of chemical information processing, and designs that make significant use of interacting virtual machines.

2. Understanding the requirements for specific designs, e.g. requirements for a human-like robot.

I think most philosophers ignore computers and computation except as providing tools to enable them to write papers, exchange email, browse the web etc. And they don't bother to learn how the machines they use are designed, implemented, debugged, and extended. One of the by-products of this neglect has been a failure

of many philosophers to understand the variety of types of information-processing architecture and the way in which different
architectures support different sets of concepts (Sloman, 2002a).
In particular, as mentioned above, many of them have no understanding of the philosophical interest of relations between virtual
machines and the underlying physical machines.[11]

This limited understanding can lead at one extreme to gross
over-simplification of the problems of explaining human and animal competences and designing machines with similar competences, and at the other extreme to a belief that the task of understanding humans and explaining how they work is far too complex
and subtle to be aided by learning about information processing,
leading to varieties of "mysterianism" often inspired by arguments
presented or reported in Chalmers (1996).

There have been many over-simplifications that result from inadequate understanding of requirements and designs, including
the spread of "symbol grounding theory"[12], even among many
people who work with computers, over-inflation of importance of
emotions for intelligent systems[13], including a failure to understand that emotions are just a subset among a large variety of
types of control process, confusions about embodiment and sit-
uatedness, exaggerating the role of sensorimotor contingencies in
cognition[14] and confusions about the relevance of Turing machines
to the long term goals of research in AI (Sloman, 2002c).

5. Open problems

Question 5: What are the most important open problems concerning computation and/or information and what are the prospects
for progress?

Importance is in the eye of the beholder. I can only talk about
what interests me, and why.

---

[11] A recent paper by John Pollock is an exception: "What am I? Virtual Machines and the Mind/Body Problem" (June 2007) http://philsci-
archive.pitt.edu/archive/00003341/, To appear in *Philosophy and Phenomenological Research*.

[12] Criticised in this presentation:
http://www.cs.bham.ac.uk/research/projects/cogaff/talks/#models

[13] As explained in this "popular" presentation:
http://www.cs.bham.ac.uk/research/projects/cogaff/talks/#cafe04

[14] As explained in
http://www.cs.bham.ac.uk/research/projects/cosy/papers/#dp0603

I think the two hardest unsolved problems are (a) specifying what vision is and how human visual capabilities can be explained, and (b) analysing the concept of causation. I have already referred to some of the unsolved problems regarding vision. I conjecture that one of the reasons why it is so difficult to come up with a satisfactory analysis of causation is that there are two concepts of causation in wide use, namely Humean causation, and Kantian causation. Kantian causal reasoning is based on information about structures and composition of physical things, and often uses the kind of spatial reasoning that got me interested in AI. Some of the things philosophers do when discussing causation, such as talking about possible worlds, can divert attention from the task of understanding what happens when individuals use their understanding of causation in the process of learning things and achieving things, in the environment. At a workshop on natural and artificial cognition in June 2007 Jackie Chappell and I gave a linked pair of presentations on varieties of causation, available online at http://www.cs.bham.ac.uk/research/projects/cogaff/talks/wonac.

Other problems still in need of investigation, include explaining how a blind robot can "grow up", as congenitally blind humans do, with a rich understanding of the spatial world, explaining what it is to be interested in something, what it is to like or dislike something, to value something, or to find something funny. My original problem of explaining how understanding of mathematics, including the development through infancy and childhood of spatial forms of reasoning alongside reasoning using Fregean forms of representation, also remains unsolved. Closely connected with this is the problem of explaining how ontologies and forms of representation develop through playful exploration of both ideas and the environment.[15]

There are more abstract problems about the diversity of sets of requirements (i.e. niches) and the diversity of designs and how feedback loops linking them can drive evolution. Understanding this fully (if that is possible) will require development of new mathematics. Other problems concern the sorts of architectures that are possible. It is very unlikely that we have an adequate characterisation of the space of information-processing architectures for intelligent systems, especially architectures that grow themselves.

There are many more unsolved problems and I am sure that re-

---

[15]http://www.cs.bham.ac.uk/research/projects/cosy/papers/#pr0604

searchers in this area will be kept busy for several more decades at least and possibly for centuries more. Confident pronouncements about how soon computer-based machines will overtake humans can safely be ignored while the problems that need to be solved are still not understood.

Perhaps the most important unsolved problem of all is how to undo the damage caused, and retrieve the opportunities lost, by all the practices in the last few decades perverting computing education in schools towards the goal of producing industry-fodder instead of attempting to stretch the creative, independent, model-building and reasoning capabilities of young minds.

Some related online papers and presentations

http://www.cs.bham.ac.uk/research/projects/cosy/papers/#tr0703
Computational Cognitive Epigenetics
http://www.cs.bham.ac.uk/research/projects/cosy/papers/#tr0705
On qualia in intelligent machines and a new kind of Turing test.
http://www.cs.bham.ac.uk/research/projects/cogaff/talks/#cafe04
Do machines, natural or artificial, really need emotions?
http://www.cs.bham.ac.uk/research/projects/cogaff/talks/wonac
Presentations on causation at Oxford workshop on natural and artificial intelligence.

References

Boden, M.A. (1978). *Artificial intelligence and natural man.* Hassocks, Sussex: Harvester Press. (Second edition 1986. MIT Press).

Boden, M.A. (2006). *Mind As Machine: A history of Cognitive Science (Vols 1–2).* Oxford: Oxford University Press.

Chalmers, D.J. (1996). *The conscious mind: In search of a fundamental theory.* New York, Oxford: Oxford University Press.

Chappell, J., & Sloman, A. (2007). Natural and artificial meta-configured altricial information-processing systems. *International Journal of Unconventional Computing*, 3(3), 211–239.
(http://www.cs.bham.ac.uk/research/projects/cosy/papers/#tr0609)

Gibson, E.J., & Pick, A.D. (2000). *An Ecological Approach to Perceptual Learning and Development.* New York: Oxford University Press.

Jablonka, E., & Lamb, M.J. (2005). *Evolution in Four Dimensions: Genetic, Epigenetic, Behavioral, and Symbolic Variation in the History of Life*. Cambridge MA: MIT Press.

Jamnik, M., Bundy, A., & Green, I. (1999). On automating diagrammatic proofs of arithmetic arguments. *Journal of Logic, Language and Information*, 8(3), 297–321.

Kant, I. (1781). *Critique of pure reason*. London: Macmillan. (Translated (1929) by Norman Kemp Smith)

McCarthy, J. (1996). *The Well Designed Child*. Stanford University.
(http://www-formal.stanford.edu/jmc/child1.html)

McCarthy, J., & Hayes, P. (1969). Some philosophical problems from the standpoint of AI. In B. Meltzer & D. Michie (Eds.), *Machine Intelligence* 4 (pp. 463–502). Edinburgh, Scotland: Edinburgh University Press.
(http://www-formal.stanford.edu/jmc/mcchay69/mcchay69.html)

Sloman, A. (1962). *Knowing and Understanding: Relations between meaning and truth, meaning and necessary truth, meaning and synthetic necessary truth*. Unpublished doctoral dissertation, Oxford University.
(http://www.cs.bham.ac.uk/research/projects/cogaff/07.html#706)

Sloman, A. (1965a). Functions and Rogators. In J. N. Crossley & M. A. E. Dummett (Eds.), *Formal Systems and Recursive Functions: Proceedings of the Eighth Logic Colloquium Oxford, July 1963* (pp. 156–175). Amsterdaim: North-Holland Publishing Co.

Sloman, A. (1965b). 'Necessary', 'A Priori' and 'Analytic'. *Analysis*, 26(1), 12–16.
(Now online http://www.cs.bham.ac.uk/research/projects/cogaff/07.html#701)

Sloman, A. (1968/9.). Explaining Logical Necessity. *Proceedings of the Aristotelian Society*, 69, 33-50.
(http://www.cs.bham.ac.uk/research/projects/cogaff/07.html#712)

Sloman, A. (1971). Interactions between philosophy and AI: The role of intuition and non-logical reasoning in intelligence. In *Proc 2nd IJCAI* (pp. 209–226). London: William Kaufmann.
(http://www.cs.bham.ac.uk/research/cogaff/04.html#200407)

Sloman, A. (1978a). *The computer revolution in philosophy*. Hassocks, Sussex: Harvester Press (and Humanities Press).
(http://www.cs.bham.ac.uk/research/cogaff/crp)

Sloman, A. (1978b). What About Their Internal Languages? Commentary on three articles by Premack, D., Woodruff, G., by Griffn, D.R., and by Savage-Rumbaugh, E.S., Rumbaugh, D.R., Boysen, S. published in Behavioral and Brain Sciences Journal 1978, 1 (4). *Behavioral and Brain Sciences,* 1(4), 515.
(http://www.cs.bham.ac.uk/research/projects/cogaff/07.html#713)

Sloman, A. (1979). The primacy of non-communicative language. In M. MacCafferty & K. Gray (Eds.), *The analysis of Meaning: Informatics 5 Proceedings ASLIB/BCS Conference, Oxford, March 1979* (pp. 1–15). London: Aslib.
(http://www.cs.bham.ac.uk/research/projects/cogaff/81-95.html#43)

Sloman, A. (1982). Image interpretation: The way ahead? In O. Braddick & A. Sleigh. (Eds.), *Physical and Biological Processing of Images (Proceedings of an international symposium organised by The Rank Prize Funds, London, 1982.)* (pp. 380–401). Berlin: Springer-Verlag.
(http://www.cs.bham.ac.uk/research/projects/cogaff/06.html#0604)

Sloman, A. (1984). Experiencing Computation: A Tribute to Max Clowes. In *New Horizons in Educational Computing Book Contents* (pp. 207–219). Ellis Horwood Series In Artificial Intelligence Archive.
(http://www.cs.bham.ac.uk/research/projects/cogaff/00-02.html#71)

Sloman, A. (1989). On designing a visual system (towards a gibsonian computational model of vision). *Journal of Experimental and Theoretical AI,* 1(4), 289–337.
(http://www.cs.bham.ac.uk/research/projects/cogaff/81-95.html#7)

Sloman, A. (1993). The mind as a control system. In C. Hookway & D. Peterson (Eds.), *Philosophy and the cognitive sciences* (pp. 69–110). Cambridge, UK: Cambridge University Press.
(http://www.cs.bham.ac.uk/research/projects/cogaff/81-95.html#18)

Sloman, A. (1994). How to design a visual system – Gibson remembered. In D.Vernon (Ed.), *Computer vision: Craft, engineering and science.* Berlin: Springer Verlag.

Sloman, A. (1995). Musings on the roles of logical and non-logical representations in intelligence. In J. Glasgow, H. Narayanan, & B. Chandrasekaran (Eds.), *Diagrammatic reasoning: Computational and cognitive perspectives* (pp. 7–33). MIT Press.

Sloman, A. (1996). Towards a general theory of representations. In D.M.Peterson (Ed.), *Forms of representation: an interdisciplinary theme for cognitive science* (pp. 118–140). Exeter, U.K.: Intellect Books.

Sloman, A. (1998, August). Diagrams in the mind. In *in Proceedings twd98 (Thinking with diagrams: Is there a science of diagrams?)* (pp. 1–9). Aberystwyth.

Sloman, A. (2001). Evolvable biologically plausible visual architectures. In T. Cootes & C. Taylor (Eds.), *Proceedings of British Machine Vision Conference* (pp. 313–322). Manchester: BMVA.

Sloman, A. (2002a). Architecture-based conceptions of mind. In *In the Scope of Logic, Methodology, and Philosophy of Science* (Vol II) (pp. 403–427). Dordrecht: Kluwer. (Synthese Library Vol. 316)

Sloman, A. (2002b). Diagrams in the mind. In M. Anderson, B. Meyer, & P. Olivier (Eds.), *Diagrammatic representation and reasoning*. Berlin: Springer-Verlag.

Sloman, A. (2002c). The irrelevance of Turing machines to AI. In M. Scheutz (Ed.), *Computationalism: New Directions* (pp. 87–127). Cambridge, MA: MIT Press.
(http://www.cs.bham.ac.uk/research/cogaff/00-02.html#77)

Sloman, A. (2006, May). *Sensorimotor vs objective contingencies* (Research Note No. COSY-DP-0603). School of Computer Science, University of Birmingham.
(http://www.cs.bham.ac.uk/research/projects/cosy/papers/#dp0603)

Sloman, A. (2007). Diversity of Developmental Trajectories in Natural and Artificial Intelligence: Technical Report FS-07-03. In C.T. Morrison & T.T. Oates (Eds.), *Computational Approaches to Representation Change during Learning and Development. AAAI. Fall Symposium 2007* (pp. 70–79). Menlo Park, CA: AAAI Press.
(http://www.cs.bham.ac.uk/research/projects/cosy/papers/#tr0704)

Sloman, A., & Chappell, J. (2005). The Altricial-Precocial Spectrum for Robots. *In Proceedings IJCAI'05* (pp. 1187–1192). Edinburgh: IJCAI.
(http://www.cs.bham.ac.uk/research/cogaff/05.html#200502)

Sloman, A., & Chappell, J. (2007). Computational Cognitive Epigenetics (Commentary on (Jablonka & Lamb, 2005)). *Behavioral and Brain Sciences*, 30(4).
(http://www.cs.bham.ac.uk/research/projects/cosy/papers/#tr0703)

Sloman, A., Chrisley, R., & Scheutz, M. (2005). The architectural basis of affective states and processes. In M. Arbib & J.-M. Fellous

(Eds.), *Who Needs Emotions?: The Brain Meets the Robot* (pp. 203–244). New York: Oxford University Press.
(http://www.cs.bham.ac.uk/research/cogaff/03.html#200305)

Trehub, A. (1991). *The Cognitive Brain.* Cambridge, MA: MIT Press.
(http://www.people.umass.edu/trehub/)

Wegner, P. (1968). *Programming Languages, Information Structures, and Machine Organization.* New York: McGraw Hill.

Wing, J. M. (2006). Computational Thinking. *CACM, 49*(3), 33–35.
(http://www.cs.cmu.edu/afs/cs/usr/wing/www/publications/Wing06.pdf)

Winterstein, D. (2005). *Using Diagrammatic Reasoning for Theorem Proving in a Continuous Domain.* Unpublished doctoral dissertation, University of Edinburgh, School of Informatics.
(http://www.era.lib.ed.ac.uk/handle/1842/642)

Wright, I., Sloman, A., & Beaudoin, L. (1996). Towards a design-based analysis of emotional episodes. *Philosophy Psychiatry and Psychology,* 3(2), 101–126.
(http://www.cs.bham.ac.uk/research/projects/cogaff/96-99.html#2)

14

Patrick Suppes

Lucie Stern Professor of Philosophy, Emeritus

Stanford University, USA

---

1. Why were you initially drawn to computational or informational issues?

I begin with some history. I am not sure just when I first thought about the use of computers for computation, but I do remember the late 1950s when Dick Atkinson and I were writing a book on applications of learning models and stimulus-response reinforcement concepts to simple game situations. The book is full of extended computations supported by use of the I.B.M. 650 Computer at Stanford, which was one of the very earliest made available to academic communities to have the possibility of going beyond the old days of computing with hand calculators. We say this in the preface of Suppes and Atkinson (1960): "Evan Linick has been indispensable in programming many problems for the I.B.M. 650 Computer at Stanford; we are also indebted to Richard Hill of the Western Data Processing Center for his cooperation." This brief acknowledgement is all we had to say about what was really a first, big-time, move into computing from my own standpoint. At that time, the only task was facilitating the many statistical estimates of parameters and the like for the models introduced in the book. It is important to realize how fundamental the change was in feasible applications of statistics with the introduction of digital computers in the 1950s. Even very simple formulations of linear-programming or linear-regression problems, that were practically unsolvable, could now be used to address all kinds of interesting questions in theories of behavior and social interaction. I was pleased to be on the initial wave of this range of applications (for those reading this that do not know much about my background, I have spent as much of my time as a scientist as I have as a philosopher.)

The next step was a significant one, and in fact an important predecessor in a long career of being concerned with the use of computers for instruction. The shift from data analysis to instruction is conceptually a big one: this direction involved a much deeper commitment to thinking about computation in many different ways. It began with something rather simple: the delivery of elementary exercises in arithmetic, mainly in the form of drill and practice, initially to students in elementary schools close to Stanford. In fact, the very first experiments began early in the 1960s when John McCarthy and I, with grants we had available, shared the expense of purchasing one of the early PDP-1's from Digital Equipment Corporation. To give a flavor of early work on computers, where we were concerned with the real-time performance for instructional purposes, I quote from an early book I co-authored on these matters (Suppes, Jerman, and Brian, 1968) recounting experiences in 1965-1966. In fact, the book's title is *Computer-Assisted Instruction: Stanford's 1965-66 Arithmetic Program*. Here is a quotation from Chapter 9 on the nature of the time-sharing system and CAI programming:

> This chapter briefly describes the operating system and programming language used to implement the drill-and-practice system. The complete process of coding, inputting, and debugging is described in connection with several examples. This description is of the operating system in effect during 1966-67, which is an improvement on that running during 1965-66. For a detailed description of the general time-sharing system in effect during 1965-66, see McCarthy et al (1967).

> The hardware used is a highly modified PDP-1 made by Digital Equipment Corporation. The PDP-1 is a small to medium-sized binary computer with 32,000 words of 5-microsecond core memory. The system operates in a general time-sharing mode.

> The heart of the time-sharing system is a 131,000 word-swapping drum. Each user program is normally read into memory in turn and allowed to run for a short period of time. Then the program is re-written on the drum and the next program is brought in. This process of interchanging two user programs from core memory to drum is known as program swapping. The process takes 32 milliseconds on the PDP-1. The new program

swapped in is commonly allowed to run for 64 milliseconds if it does not create some situation causing it to be terminated early. Normal early terminations will consist of things such as waiting for input or output to be completed. For example, if a program tries to read a keyboard but there has been no input on the keyboard, the program will be dismissed until the input becomes available. A program so terminated will not be swapped into memory until the cause for its termination is removed. When input which was unavailable becomes available, the program is marked active and is put back in line to be run when its turn comes.

To introduce the system response cycle, we take as an example a program which reads input (such as checking for a correct single character answer to a question), and then responds with some output to the teletype. The period from the time the key is struck until the printer responds with the next message from the program is known as the system response time. This time should be fast enough to give a human user the impression that there was little or no system response time. This system response time can be compared with response times in devices such as automatic self-service elevators and telephones (for example, dial or busy tones). A system response time longer than 1-2 seconds will create impatience and disinterest, and will be very annoying to users.

The 131D data channel is connected to an IBM 1301 model II random-access disk file. The total capacity of this file is on the order of 336 million bits (56 million 6-bit characters of 18-1/2 million 18-bit words). Two independent-access arms are provided.

Maximum seek (arm movement) time is 180 milliseconds. When the appropriate arm is positioned there is a rotational delay of 0-34 milliseconds before the transfer may begin. The average delay is 17 milliseconds. The transfer rate is one 18-bit word about every 35 microseconds or every seventh memory cycle. The rate is comparable with that of high-speed magnetic tape drives. However, the relatively fast random access has a very distinct advantage over (serial-access) magnetic tape units in a time-sharing environment, because of the rapid switching between user programs and hence between users' files (Suppes, Jerman, and Brian, 1968, pp. 291-92).

These paragraphs seem really quaint forty years later. Just about every computing device, including current cell phones, has more computer power than we had available then. There is more progress between the PDP-1 and current computer facilities widely available than there is between the earlier introduction of the Model-T Ford in the 1920s and current automobiles, a much more radical conceptual evolution over a much shorter period.

Notice however, that I am still concerned here with using computers to deliver a product that is different, of course, than it could ever be delivered by other means, but still delivered as a rather standard product. To emphasize how differences are possible, I stress that the important psychological measure of response latency (i.e. the time it takes for a student to make each response), can be measured and studied carefully, something that is not possible in the classroom or even, really, by an individual tutor with no computer facilities. I can elaborate on this point, but will not here.

In any case, practical involvement with computers had its theoretical consequences, however, and during the 1960s my thinking about many conceptual questions relevant to computing changed forever. One of the things I got involved in was the controversy between behaviorists and cognitivists, or linguists such as Noam Chomsky, on the nature of the mind, about which more in answer to the next question.

2.What examples from your work (or the work of others) best illustrate the fruitful use of computational and/or informational approach for foundational researches and/or applications?

The appearance of Chomsky's famous review (1959) of Skinner's *Verbal Behavior* (1957), marked a change that proved permanent in the acceptance of behaviorism, in particular the learning theory, of the stimulus-response variety that was dominant in American psychology from the 1920s to the latter part of the 1950s. Skinner's *Verbal Behavior*, with its non-mathematical formulation, but with rather strong claims made in much too qualitative and vague a way, was an easy target for Chomsky's detailed critique. One of the primary effects was to disturb, again in a way that was a permanent change, the theoretical complacency of many behavioral psychologists.

Since I followed this development rather closely, because of my attempts with Bill Estes and others to give a sharp mathematical formulation of stimulus-response theory, I was sometimes called "the white knight of behaviorism". Very early in the 1960s, I remember a famous public debate I had on these questions with Chomsky at Stanford. The aisles were crowded, there was no place to sit down, the students were enthralled, not because of me, but because of Chomsky. I enjoyed it, and so did Noam, who can sometimes be rather rude and impolite in controversy, but certainly not on the present occasion. We argued vigorously, but with respect for each other, and although we have not been in contact much for many years, I think if we had a debate today, it would have the same tone, even if the discussion took a rather different turn.

Many of the new breed of cognitive psychologists took Chomsky's criticism and what followed as devastating in showing the utter inadequacy of stimulus-response theory as a theory of behavior. Of course, these claims and conclusions, as is often the case in such scientific debates, were supported neither by careful mathematical argument to show that, in principle, a conceptual inadequacy is to be found in all standard stimulus-response theories, nor by systematic presentation of empirical evidence to show that the basic assumptions of these theories are empirically false. As I said at the time, "To cite two recent books of some importance, neither theorems nor data are to be found in Chomsky (1965) or Katz and Postal (1964), but rather one can find many useful examples of linguistic analysis, many interesting and insightful remarks about language behavior, and many incompletely worked out arguments about theories of language learning" (Suppes, 1969, pp. 327-328). The article in which I made these general remarks was one in which I proved that, in a clear mathematical sense, it was possible to give a stimulus-response theory of finite automata. The fundamental theorem is that given any connected finite automaton, there is a stimulus-response model that asymptotically becomes isomorphic to it. Moreover, the stimulus-response model may have all responses initially unconditioned. Looking back on this, I am still happy with the paper, and the proof is, of course, still correct. I had some arguments about it, and a good account of those arguments and my detailed responses are to be found in Suppes (2002, Chapter 8). It is not the point here to enter into details, but there are two remarks I want to make. First, objections to the fact that finite automaton are only good for the processing or parsing of regular languages, and not context-free ones, is an irrelevancy in a debate of this kind. Clearly, any model that processes real language handled by real people is finite and not infinite in character. It is only an idle abstraction to think in terms of the actual requirement of infinite storage for parsing or producing utterances of an arbitrary context-free language.

The second and more important point is that it was not realized, and in my own mind is still not realized by many cognitive scientists, that the apparatus required for universal computation is extremely simple in nature. I have in mind any of various characterizations of computational devices equivalent to universal Turing machines. Perhaps the best universal Turing machine which is easy to describe is the one of Marvin Minsky's that has a language of four symbols and seven internal states (it is a nice criterion for the simplicity of Turing machines to take the multiple of the number of symbols and the number of states required as a measure of its elementary character.) But, other related computational ideas can be used, such as those of register machines or Church's lambda calculus. The point is the apparatus is simple; however, the proof that such simple apparatus is adequate to compute any computable function, that is, any partial recursive function, is not so simple. So, it is easy enough in stimulus-response theory, therefore, to construct a simple computing device adequate under the usual ideal circumstances to universal computing.

I am happy to say that the inadequate computational ideas of the cognitive psychologists of the late 1960s and 1970s were soon displaced by modern connectionism, which is itself a close relative of classical stimulus-response theory. But my general intellectual spirit is irenic enough to concede that the cognitivists made a number of good shifts of focus, to new sets of questions, which probably would not have been studied without their impetus. I can say other gracious things of this kind, but it is more important to move on given the limited space available for these rather large topics to my current main interest in computation conceptually.

Since 1996, after my retirement in 1992 at 70, I have been very much involved in brain experiments, especially with EEG (Electroencephalographic) recordings of brain activity. There is, of course, not enough time to go into all that. Here I will restrict myself to saying that having now spent over ten years in fairly intensive experimentation on the cognitive nature of brain processes, I see something different from the computational paradigms of early decades is required to move to the right conception of brain computations. The ones that I am interested in have three characteristics. First, they all seem to be electromagnetic in character, because they are system computations, not computations of individual cells, which are often chemical in nature. Second, they are without doubt conceptually to be thought of probabilistically, given the complicated physical environment in which they take place. And third, they seem to be deeply parallel in structure, a stage we are just coming to in modern digital computing, but which will undoubtedly be a major focus for the 21st century. The PCs now being produced have several multiple cores, which mean they are ready for parallel processing, and those multiple cores will rapidly increase in number. But without doubt, full and adequate use of their blazing computational power will be constrained by the comparatively slow development of adequate parallel software.

So what I have said here about the brain is a way of saying indirectly that I am skeptical of the earlier attempt to use digital computers as a model of the mind, a topic that is not so popular now and for good reason.

There is another aspect of computation that I think has perhaps been undervalued in foundational work. The broad-scale introduction of modern computers into all the nooks and crannies of academic life have provided a wonderful illustration of the relevancy of formalism. The formal program in the foundations of mathematics, initiated in the latter half of the 19th century by Pasch, Frege, Hilbert, and others, seems far removed from practical kinds of thinking, even from purely theoretical reflections on thinking. Certainly the ordinary mentalese used by philosophers in talking about the mind had little place for formalism. But computers have shown how useful and important such formalisms are, and at the same time, the awkwardness of the rigid character of formal languages is something that is recognized by all. There has been a big push in many ways to get away from the formal approach to computer languages. In fact, I would even say that one of the foundational things that has been made clear by modern computing, in the struggle to build interfaces for spoken natural languages between user and computer, is how much more difficult a problem it is than it seems at first. I mistakenly and optimistically predicted in the 1960s, in an article of mine on the use of computers in education (1966), that in 30 or 40 years computers would be doing the work of a modern Socrates in full-scale dialogue with students on nearly any subject they might choose. How foolish that was. We still do not have even one serviceable operating system that uses spoken language in its natural form as a main form of computer interaction. Surely, to make once again a forecast, this will be one of the outcomes of the 21st century, and in my own judgment, the greatest revolution that will be coming along in the relation between our digital devices and ourselves. It is only when we can have easy and natural conversations that we will begin to think about computers in a really different way. (The future of robotic sex I will not try to forecast.) So, from a general foundational standpoint, it is that need for computers that are sophisticated enough in their structure and function to conduct such conversations in a meaningful way, especially in terms of responding in such a way as to have a natural psychological feeling.

3. What is the proper role of computer science and/or information science in relation to other disciplines?

I draw a distinction in answering this question between the use of computers and computer science. There is no doubt that almost all the sciences are saturated with the use of computers, but as in the case of most scientific disciplines, the detailed nuances of current research in computer science are not directly absorbed into other disciplines, either in the natural or social sciences, even though the overwhelming central role of computers in both the natural and social sciences will surely continue.

Of course, what I have just said is too simple. The results of computer science turn up in applications sometime later. I say this with something specific in mind: outside of practitioners who engage in continual data analysis, it is difficult to accept how saturated large parts of science are now with superb computer programs for calculations that would have been impossible even in much of the 20th century – the large-scale statistical programs, the many different parts of Math Lab, Mathematica, and Maple, just to mention some of the most familiar and most used programs. These computational facilities create conceptual revolutions in scientific disciplines that rely heavily on computation – this includes mathematics too. A good example is mathematical statistics. The main topics of statistics have been changed in ways hard to believe over the past two or three decades. What was known as modern statistics in the 20th century, the extensive mathematical development of hypothesis testing and estimation of parameters, has been replaced by a whole battery of new techniques concerned with very large data sets and machine-learning approaches to finding significant relationships in them. So, another way of answering this question would be to emphasize that, in this case, we have a conceptual change resulting from the sheer change in quantity of data and of simulation of data, as in Monte Carlo simulations of theoretical models. I have no doubt that this shift, which was not a quick one but took place over several decades, will be one of the important conceptual changes in the nature of science remarked upon in a very general way in the future, and will be attributed to changes in computational possibilities, and thereby changes in the nature of theories, models, and concepts studied in many parts of science.

4. What do you consider the most neglected topics and/or contributions in late 20th century studies of computation and/or information?

The topic that I mention for most neglected is one that actually has a long scientific history, but glimmerings of new developments have opened up and are yet to be fully absorbed, either in individual sciences or in the broad, philosophical attitudes to science. I have in mind new and deeper conceptions of the nature of error or variability. It has been recognized since the 18th century, with work that began at least with Simpson, and was followed, mainly independently, by many people, including especially Gauss, that a quantitative theory of error is essential to quantitative science. The essence of the systematic development of quantitative theories of error is one of the surprising omissions of ancient astronomy, where such a concept could have been used, in spite of the lack of quantitative refinement of observations. There are many places in Ptolemy's *Almagest* where he discusses problems of error of observation, but nowhere is there an attempt to move to a quantitative analysis. But, beginning with the renaissance of astronomy in the 16th and 17th centuries, by the 18th century the need for such a theory was well recognized, and had already in some ways been initialized by Newton, so that the systematic development of methods such as that of least mean squares to estimate errors by Gauss and others, and to develop a probabilistic treatment as well, was one of the main triumphs of the 19th century in probability and statistics. I do not know the exact date, but it was some time during the middle of the 19th century that it became routine to compute mean-square-error terms for astronomical observations, and to report them in the journals. Since then, it has become a fact of life for all students in the natural sciences, and the social sciences as well.

There has also been a major contribution from quantum mechanics in the first half of the 20th century, the discussion of which is often built around Heisenberg's principle of uncertainty. One formulation of which is that theoretically, in measuring position and momentum of a particle, the product of the error terms as expressed by the variances of the distributions of the measurements, cannot be reduced below a positive fixed lower bound. This important conceptual result at the center of the early development of quantum mechanics, also represents a reversal of the idealized conceptual thinking of 19th century classical physics, which preferred conceptualizing errors as being able to be reduced to ever smaller quantities by appropriate improved measurement procedures. There was, in the rich and important development of physics in the 19th century, no serious effort to claim that there must be, in principle, limits to the elimination of error.

We now have other new and important theoretical results about error, or variability – remember, the qualitative explanation of quantum mechanical errors of measurement are properly attributed to the impossibility of not interacting with a quantum particle when measuring it. What came to be realized is that measurement is a physical process, not an imaginary one. The actual effort of measurement requires energy and disturbs in some way the object or process being measured. One of the striking extensions of these ideas to a far-ranging theoretical result is to be found in the beautiful results of ergodic theory by Donald Ornstein and Bernard Weiss (1991) in something as classical as billiards. When a rigid convex object is placed in the middle of a billiard table, the classical, physical model of billiards deterministic to the core, together with necessary errors of measurement, cannot be distinguished from a purely stochastic model of the motion of the billiard ball. This kind of example is a vivid one, but the results can easily be extended to related systems having similar ergodic properties, which we naturally associate with chaos. The two theories – the classical and the stochastic – are, of course, mathematically inconsistent taken together. But the important point of the Ornstein and Weiss theorem is that no matter how many observations are taken, as long as they are finite in number, it is not possible to distinguish between the classical physical model with errors of measurement, and a stochastic Markov model. Put in more general terms, the data do not permit us to distinguish between a theoretical deterministic model and an indeterministic one (Suppes, 1993).

This discussion of Ornstein and Weiss' work actually has a much broader philosophical setting, that goes back to some of the most famous antimonies introduced in philosophy, namely the antimonies of Kant in his *Critique of Pure Reason* (Suppes, 1995). It is especially the causal Third Antimony that is relevant here. The thesis is about spontaneous events breaking the causal change and the antithesis affirms uniform causal determinism for all of nature. The proofs of the thesis and the antithesis of the Antimony proceed by proving the source of the paradox in the absurdity of the other view. Kant's own analysis locates the source of the paradox in the unconditional nature of the antimonies. As is already evident, I favour the resolution offered by the empirical indistinguishability of theories, deterministic on the one hand and indeterministic on the other, arising from such conceptual results as those of Ornstein and Weiss. The paradox arises only with the assumption of perfection – that is that continuous physical quantities, or other such observable properties, can be measured with unlimited precision. It is easy to say, "Well this is simply not possible in practice," but in principle, is another matter. The important point in clarifying the conceptual confusion that arises from Kant's rightly celebrated Antimony is that there is a genuine problem here. The empirical, but in principle, solution you get from accepting the inevitability of errors of measurement or variability in the environment, bounded away from zero, is yet to be widely recognized as a real resolution of philosophical significance. (My praise of the importance of Kant's Antimonies does not mean that I support his own resolution of them, but that is another story.)

There is no space to mention other neglected topics in the late 20th century in any detail, but I will cite one that I consider of great importance, and that is the relatively slow development of rich forms of parallel processing, important both to scientific computing and, as remarked already, to the theory of brain computation.

5. What are the most important open problems concerning computation and/or information and what are the prospects for progress?

It is not difficult to construct a long list of important open problems, but I shall restrict myself to just two. The first concerns the fundamental nature of physical space and time. The just discussed ergodic results of Ornstein and Weiss about our inability to discriminate between deterministic physics and stochastic physics for billiard balls, also applicable to other scientific theories, should lead to new conceptions of space and time. Physicists have not, by and large, accepted the strong smoothness conditions of mathematicians for standard formulations of space and time. But there is still a reluctance to develop what seems to be a natural isomorphism between discrete space-time and continuous space-time. Of course, this approach is natural only when extremely small, discrete, grids of space and time are accepted. But once this kind of thinking begins, it seems intuitive and the way things ought to be. In this case, there is an antimony of Kant's, namely the Second Antimony, the one whose thesis is that composite substances are atomistic (discrete) or the antithesis, infinitely divisible (continuous).

The smoothest conditions of classical physics were conceptually necessary in the 19th century, when there were no computers to do massive calculations and conditions needed to be imposed that worked well in the framework of classical analysis. The story, more than a hundred years later, is very different. Most large-scale physical models are computed discretely, that is, through discrete numerical approximations on standard digital computers, from fast PCs to supercomputers. My own forecast is that in many parts of science, and in corresponding parts of the philosophy of science, we should see in the 21st century a thorough exploration of this natural equivalence between the discrete and continuous, and therefore the proper resolution of Kant's Second Antimony when the grid of discreteness is appropriately small.

The other open problem of computation, of great importance from my standpoint, is parallel processing, as already mentioned, but especially, as also already mentioned, its part in the theory of brain computation. It had been a feature of the philosophy of mind forever not to enter into any computations of a serious nature. And yet the most casual survey of what the brain is doing, and what has been discovered experimentally, shows how the brain is to be properly looked upon as a computational device hard at work at all times, even when we are asleep. It is probably true that much of this brain power is spent processing perceptions. It is ironic how little attention has been paid to perceptual computations in the rather tortured history of the role of perception in epistemology and related parts of philosophy. Of course, perception is not the whole show, just perhaps the biggest part in terms of computation, even for humans, and certainly for most animals. There are also the computations needed for memory, for learning, and the closely related topics of generalization and concept formation. The neuroscience literature on these matters is already large, but still it is evident that we have scarcely yet reached anything like a fundamental understanding of any major part of the brain's computations. Here I am formulating this problem in terms of what is called system neuroscience: how large collections of synchronized neurons are computing. There is a similar large, complicated and impressive literature on the computations of individual cells and the signalling between them.

It is not possible to enter into an assessment of what is currently known about brain computations in any detail in this setting, but there is a point that I think is probably correct of a very general nature, and that I want to emphasize: this is that the computations of the brain are physically complex, and will only be thoroughly understood by grappling in detail with the relevant physics, and possibly chemistry. The point is that any easy, direct route to a satisfactory pure "software" formulation of brain computations seems highly unlikely. How we represent, as objects of computation, words, perceptual images, visual, auditory, tactile, and the like, are mysteries only as yet touched upon, but certainly not solved. Contrary to what I am conjecturing, it might be thought that we really will not need very much physics or chemistry for this work; we will be able to develop an abstract theory of brain computation in the way in which we already have a large development of such computations and, especially algorithms, for digital computers. It does not mean that at some point the people who design computers, large or small, do not need to know what they are doing physically: they certainly do. But those of us using the devices for computation, using the kind of sophisticated programs already mentioned, do not really have to know any physics at all to understand how to use them. My conjecture is that at least for a long time this will not be true of brain computations; we will not have a successful, general, abstract theory of brain computations as pure software, but we will be working hard for some time to untangle the physical processes of computation. And until we understand these physical processes in detail, we will not understand the computations. This is a conjecture I would like to be wrong about. Optimists will say "Surely you are;" pessimists will say, "Not at all, how could we expect it to be otherwise?"

References

Chomsky, N. (1959). Review of B.F. Skinner, *Verbal behavior.* *Language* 35: 26–58.

Chomsky, N. (1965). *Aspects of the theory of syntax.* Cambridge, Massachusetts: M.I.T. Press.

Kant, I. (1781/1997). *Critique of pure reason.* New York: Cambridge University Press. First published in 1781. Translated by P. Guyer and A.W. Wood.

Katz, J.J., and Postal, P.M. (1964). *An integrated theory of linguistic descriptions.* Cambridge, Massachusetts: M.I.T. Press.

McCarthy, et al. (1967). THOR – a display based time sharing system. *Proceedings of the 1967 Spring Joint Computer Conference,* pp. 623–633.

Ornstein, D.S. and B. Weiss (1991). Statistical properties of chaotic systems. *Bulletin of the American Mathematical Society* 24: 11–116.

Ptolemy, C. (1984). *The almagest.* New York: Springer. Translated and annotated by G. J. Toomer. Written about 150 A.D.

Skinner, B.F. (1957). *Verbal behavior.* New York: Appleton.

Suppes, P. (1966). The uses of computers in education. *Scientific American* 215: 206-220.

Suppes, P. (1969). Stimulus-response theory of finite automata. *Journal of Mathematical Psychology* 6: 327–355.

Suppes, P. (1993). The transcendental character of determinism. In P.A. French, T.E. Uehling, and H.K. Wettstein, eds., *Midwest studies in philosophy, vol. XVIII,* pages 242-57. Notre Dame, IN: University of Notre Dame Press.

Suppes, P. (1995). Transzendentale Prinzipien: eine Neubetrachtung der Kantschen Antinomien. *Metaphysik* 11: 43–54.

Suppes, P. (2002). *Representation and invariance of scientific structures.* Stanford, CA: CSLI Publications.

Suppes, P. and Atkinson, R.C. (1960). *Markov learning models for multiperson interactions.* Stanford, CA: Stanford University Press.

Suppes, P., Jerman M., and Brian, D. (1968). *Computer-assisted Instruction: Stanford's 1965-66 arithmetic program.* New York: Academic Press.

15

Johan van Benthem

Professor of Logic and its Applications
University of Amsterdam, The Netherlands
Professor of Philosophy
Stanford University, USA

---

1. Why were you initially drawn to computational and/or informational issues?

Frankly, the term 'information' had a softish ring in my student days. It was associated with Dutch philosophers writing shallow pamphlets about Everything with a soup of half-digested bits and pieces of Shannon's information theory. Nor did 'computation' have an immediate, inspiring appeal. It suggested a drill in decision methods, or an auxiliary task of implementation like writing a computer program – while its cognate 'calculating' was even decidedly objectionable. But over time, I have come to love our Editor's two themes: partly through developments in my own field of logic, and also through the rise of the discipline of *computer science*. The latter term is still somewhat unfortunate, as it suggests a dance around machines, and an auxiliary crowd of mechanics greasing wheels and serving customers. But what I have in mind is the austere Latin term "Informatica", still used in The Netherlands for the field. That has the ring of the fundamental scientific study of information, it sounds like a classy relative of "logica", and from the start, it associates with computation, a link which the questions of this interview keep alive in English with a valiant host of slashes /. All this is why I also like the modern term *Informatics*, which suggests the right mixture of themes. Enough of terminology now, and on to ideas!

I became a logician at an early age – and our field seems information-laden from the start. We tell students that valid logical inferences 'unpack the information' in given data, and in modern dynamic logics, we show them how events of observation and communication 'update the information' of rational agents. Indeed, an embarrassment of riches threatens. There are many different notions of information in logic, ranging from more deductive to more semantic views: a diversity to which I will return below. But even so, the curious thing is this. Logic has official definitions for its central concepts of proof, computation, truth, or definability, but not of information! And somehow, many logicians feel this is significant. We do not need this popular notion in the mechanics or even the foundations of our formal systems – or, as Laplace said to Napoleon, who inquired into the absence of God in his *Mécanique Céleste*: "Sire, je n'avais pas besoin de cette hypothèse".

One important push taking information more seriously was that of Jon Barwise and John Perry around 1983, who created 'situation semantics' as a radical alternative to the ancient régime in philosophical and mathematical logic. On their view, triggered by developments in cognitive psychology and philosophical epistemology, logic should study the information available in rich distributed environments (with both physical and human components), and the resulting information flow. At the same time, with a band of allies, Barwise and Perry started the 'Center for the Study of Language and Information' at Stanford, which quickly became a hot-bed of lively interdisciplinary encounters between philosophers, computer scientists, linguists, and psychologists. *CSLI* still exists today. Academic paradigms are like religions: the faithful do not just want rousing sermons and moving ceremonies, but also imposing architecture. Many still worship at the Stanford temple, though few have become out-and-out situation theorists.

At the same time, in Europe the study of natural language semantics underwent an informational turn. Jeroen Groenendijk and Martin Stokhof introduced information of language users in defining meanings of key linguistic constructions, including dynamic speech acts like questions. With Peter van Emde Boas, a pioneer in the study of parallels between natural and programming languages, and Frank Veltman, who had developed an update semantics for conditional expressions, they redefined meaning as 'potential for information update' based on abstract computation in appropriate state spaces. Similar ideas were found in the influential discourse representation theory of Irene Heim and Hans Kamp. By 1986, all this had become so natural that we started an 'Institute for Language, Logic and Information' *ITLI* in Amsterdam, which is still in full swing today. Incidentally, terminological 'capitalism' mattered even then. In 1991, *ITLI* was renamed to *ILLC*, the *Institute for Logic, Language, and Computation*, as colleagues felt that the *I* of 'information' was soft, while a *C* of 'computation' suggested depth and real labour. While we were at it, around 1990, with like-minded colleagues across Europe, we also set up the European Association for Logic, Language and Information *FoLLI*: no *C* there, though it does incorporate interfaces with computer science. *FoLLI's* annual ESSLLI Summer Schools have become a tradition traveling all over the continent. I hope that one day, just as the 'Olympic Games' transcended their Greek roots, they will travel all over the world.

Just to be sure, a serious interest in logical theories of information does not force a break with the tradition: one can also use classical tools. Around 1990, I became interested in uses of *modal logic*, my first and maybe still my truest love, as a general theory of process structure. This had to do with interests in process equivalence, expressive power, and computational complexity – but also: information! Modal logic seems well-suited as a calculus of information – and that at two levels, which reflect the tandem with computation in this Volume. First, possible worlds can represent information that agents have: witness the 'information stages' of intuitionistic logic or the 'information ranges' of epistemic logic. But second, dynamic processes of inference, observation, or communication continually *change* these static representations. And modal logic can describe those, too. Statics and dynamics come together in modern logics of what may be called *intelligent interaction* – and this is no coincidence. Logics of information should take the systematic Tandem View that information cannot be understood in isolation from the processes which convey and transforms it. *No information without transformation!* And this is not just a slogan. The *Handbook of Modal Logic* (Elsevier, Amsterdam 2006) provides some powerful machinery, and illustrations of how this methodology works in many settings.

The Tandem View shows particularly well in modern *epistemic logic*, one major strand in logical studies of information. Epistemic logic was proposed by Hintikka in philosophy in the 1960s, and independently by Aumann in economics in the 1970s. Since the 1980s, when Joe Halpern and his colleagues at *IBM* San Jose started the *TARK* conferences on Reasoning about Knowledge and Rationality, the field has flowered at the interface of computer science, philosophy, and economics. *TARK* has been one more major influence putting information on the map in logic. But one must be down to earth. Modern epistemic logic is not an account of the philosopher's Holy Grail of 'True Knowledge', whose demands are so strict that no mortal can ever aspire to it – but rather one of the more mundane, but also much more useful, notion 'to the best of my current information'.

In the 1990s, a further notable new force was the rise of 'Informatics': a new academic conglomerate of disciplines sharing a natural, not funding-driven, interest in information and computation as themes cutting through old boundaries between the humanities, social, and natural sciences. C.P. Snow deplored, but did not heal, the divide between the 'Two Cultures': Informatics is a seismic force which can redraw academic territories. By now, there are Informatics faculties in Bloomington and Edinburgh, to name a few. We still lack one in Amsterdam, though The Dream is still alive in many hearts and minds.

Thus, information and computation have been major forces in shaping my own intellectual development, my interactions with others, and even my organizational activities. Here you might wonder: why mention the latter in an interview like this? Well, I find it hard to separate individual research from interactions with colleagues and students. My current work on logics of games even intensifies an awareness of these social aspects and the intellectual power of interaction. But I even find it hard to separate this research interest from community-building activities. Call the latter the road of easy money and power if you like (before you have tried to run an institute), or the thankless life of public service (after you have). Either way, information and computation are powerful concepts that, to me and others, call irresistibly, not just for reflection, but also for broader academic action.

2. What example(s) from your work (or the work of others) best illustrates the fruitful use of a computational and/or informational approach for foundational researches and/or applications?

I am not sure what 'foundational' means in this setting, but let me mention some examples that seem important to me. First, a focus on information and computation goes far beyond the immediate necessities of signal engineering or computer programming. And I am not primarily interested in the penetration of computing technology and *ICT* into our society. But as it happens, this technology also comes with a genuine flow of deep new ideas. Informatics offers new ways of conceptualizing scientific questions

- and in doing so, it redraws boundaries in Academia in benefi-
cial ways. We saw already how casting language users as information-processing agents has reshaped linguistics and philosophical
epistemology. Here, computation starts as a pretty metaphor, but
it then runs deep. Techniques for modeling and calculating which
have been developed for the narrower purposes of programming
digital computers, turn out to work just as well, when understood
at an appropriate level of abstraction, for tasks such as grasping meanings, engaging in successful communication, or planning
intelligent interaction.

Many colleagues have contributed decisively here, not just those
mentioned so far. Peter Gärdenfors' pioneering work in the 1980s
on belief revision showed how a central process in scientific methodology but also domestic human cognition, viz. mechanisms of *self-
correction* on the basis of new information, involves precise structures of a computational nature. More broadly, 'logical AI' in
the tradition of John McCarthy merged narrower issues in computer science with essential questions of understanding the world
of *common sense* which have exercised people in the humanities
and social sciences. In the same spirit, Dov Gabbay has taken
informational-computational viewpoints across a wide range of
topics, including argumentation, temporal reasoning, or the ab-
ductive formation of new hypotheses. But one can equally well
cite Samson Abramsky's recent computational analysis of quantum mechanics using compositional modeling of programs by linear *logic games* in a category-theoretic setting. And these computational models are crossing over to cognitive science. For example, around 2000, various people (including, in different ways,
Reinhard Blutner, Michiel van Lambalgen, and Hannes Leitgeb)
have shown that computation-based default reasoning is close to
the working of *neural networks*, perhaps even that of the human
brain – thereby laying to rest sterile polemics between logic-based
and neuroscience based approaches to reasoning. My final example concerns a different part of Academia once more, viz. Rohit
Parikh's program of *social software*. This is an ambitious attempt
at applying computational-informational thinking to the analysis
and design of actual social procedures, the glue that holds society
together. This links up with game theory, social choice theory, and
other parts of the social sciences, as well as with cognitive science.
Thus, information and computation have a fundamental impact
across our universities. In all the examples mentioned, it seems
fair to say that this stance transforms existing fields, giving them

a richer set of tools, new friends, and even more importantly, a much richer agenda of significant questions to address.

My own work may also help illustrate how informatics emerges. At the 1987 Logic Colloquium in Granada, I presented a paper 'Semantic Parallels in Natural Language and Computation'. It shows how then new computational ideas like 'circumscription' make sense in linguistics, while 'abstract data types' revitalize old studies of empirical theories in the philosophy of science. And in line with the earlier Tandem View, it presents a modal logic of information stages together with informational processes of update, contraction, and revision over these. While this was still largely programmatic, my favourite vehicle for pursuing this concretely has become *epistemic logic*, suitably understood.

Let's first consider statics. Epistemic logic encodes a natural intuition of *information as range*, viz. all those worlds which one's current candidates for the actual state of affairs. Knowledge as 'to the best of my current information' then quantifies universally: an agent knows what is true in all her current candidates. To a logician, this at once raises an issue. What about the other natural, existentially quantified, idea of knowledge as 'having some piece of *evidence* for a proposition'? In a lecture at *TARK* 1993, I proposed merging range and evidence views into one calculus. Exciting combinations have appeared since, such as Dov Gabbay's 'labeled deductive systems' and Sergei Artemov's 'logic of proofs'. Thus, information has many natural aspects – and one wants to know if it is just a loose family of concepts, or whether it supports deeper links and combinations between these.

Next, my book *Exploring Logical Dynamics* (1996) tried to unify achievements by many people putting cognitive actions at centre stage as first-class citizens in logical theory. This 'Dynamic Turn' included belief revision theory, dynamic semantics, discourse representation, and other research lines in computer science, linguistics, and philosophy. The book showed that modal logic, with its nice balance between expressive power and computational complexity of languages, can unify theories of processes and information. In doing so, new themes arose. In particular, modal semantics becomes a probe to analyze existing logics into 'core' versus 'wrappings'. And then, interpreting first-order predicate logic over modal state spaces, a surprise occurred. One discovers a decidable core calculus of sequential procedures starting from assignments of objects to variables and testing of atomic facts. Standard Tarski semantics wraps this in a special structure theory of 'full assignment spaces' – which leads to the usual undecidability. What the modal models add here is a deeper understanding of the phenomenon of *dependence* between variables. This suggests an alternative view of *information as correlation*: but more on that below.

Around 2000, Willem Groeneveld, Jelle Gerbrandy and Hans van Ditmarsch finished their dissertations on information update in epistemic logic, while Alexandru Baltag visited ILLC as a postdoc. Since then, there has been a development of *dynamic epistemic logics* providing a super-structure to static logics of information by also describing information-carrying actions and events explicitly, with concrete procedures updating current epistemic models. Thus, the Tandem View lives inside one logical system. Recently, with students and colleagues, I have extended this approach to deal with belief revision by changing doxastic plausibility relations over models, and even to changes in agents' preferences. Dynamic epistemic logic is a framework for modeling information in observed events, but also an axiomatic calculus for such scenarios, with crucial 'dynamic system equations' telling us which information agents have after which events. A natural next step here also takes in agents' goals in acquiring and processing information, 'making sense' of the flow. With that, we get into *games* and *strategic interaction* over time. 'Logic and Games' is a lively information and computation-related current research area which is shaping up these days, but it is the topic of my interview in another *Five Questions* volume. One may even claim that information makes most sense in longer-term interaction – witness Keith Devlin's tongue-in-cheek definition of information as 'the ping-pong ball of communication'.

But there is much more to the relation of logic and information. With Pieter Adriaans, professor of learning systems in Amsterdam, I am editing a *Handbook of the Philosophy of Information*. By accident, it fell upon me to write the chapter on 'Logical Theories of Information', together with Maricarmen Martinez. Here is a summary of its conclusion:

Logic as theory of information is a legitimate perspective which puts many things in an attractive new light. One now pursues statics and dynamics, with intertwined accounts of information structure and dynamic processes that manipulate it. Thus, epistemic logic is an information theory of *range, knowledge*, and *observation-based update*. In doing so, we encounter the essential role of agents, and how they take information: often in interaction with others. But there is another basic aspect of information, its 'aboutness' and its links to the reality that we are interested in. Situation theory focuses on *correlation* and *dependence* between different parts of distributed systems. This is a complementary view of how agents access information in a structured world, and why it is there for them to pick up and communicate in the first place. The situation-theoretic perspective is not in conflict with the epistemic one, but rather a natural complement. But logic even offers a third major view, now more syntactic, of *information as code,* in the form of proof systems and other syntax-based calculi that drive inferential processes of *elucidation.* At this third stage, we link up with information processing as computation, and quantitative views of information. There are significant issues of compatibility and co-operation between all these views, and we have merely indicated some merges, leaving the question if a Grand Unification is desirable, or even possible, to others.

3. What is the proper role of computer science and/or information science in relation to other disciplines?

It seems hard to say what computer or information science is, as practitioners do not agree among themselves. In The Netherlands, the field has a history of ideological quarrels and lack of a united front to the outside world. Even base curricula change dramatically over time, as if there is no common treasury of consolidated insights. With this caveat out of the way, and sticking to my favourite term of 'Informatics', here is what I would say.

Information and computation are a new focus of research with a flavour like physics since the 17th century: scientific thought for professionals and technological innovation in society go hand in hand. While computers are changing our social world, computer scientists are changing academia. I will focus on the latter's *cultural role,* which is a social one, too, provided fundamental insights make their way outside in an appropriate manner.

Starting from the 1930s, informatics has produced a steady stream of new notions and insights, which affect the way we conceptualize problems across the university. The start was spectacular with Turing machines, which made computation a mathematical notion, with deep results such as the undecidability of natural questions like the Halting Problem. Over time, the study of computation generated further powerful ideas, which – de-coupled from their initial practical setting – turned out to have wide applicability. Examples are Automata Theory, Complexity Theory,

Semantics of Programs, Type Theory and Linear Logic, Process Theory, Data Base Theory, Artificial Intelligence, and the list is growing still. These topics show a natural unity, in that they track the growing sophistication and sweep of a joint study of representation of data plus methods of computation over these. Just consider a few examples. The work by Dijkstra and Hoare in the 1960s on the effects of structured sequential programs run on single computers led to the *dynamic logic* of Salwicki, Pratt, and others, a general paradigm for describing actions and events which has found its way as far as linguistics and philosophy. Around 1980, distributed systems and parallel computation on many computers posed a new challenge. Here, a major innovation was the work of Milner and others on *process algebra,* which is now a general theory of communicating processes reaching out as far as physics and biology . And computation continues to inspire new fundamental theory. Just look at the *co-algebra* of Aczel and others, the study of never-ending computation over infinite data streams, which cannot be constructed, only observed. Co-algebra already has repercussions for mathematical proof methods in analysis and set theory. Finally, consider the realities of the Internet. This is best described as a mixed society of human and virtual agents engaging in interactions like those of ordinary life – cooperating at times, but also competing for scarce resources. Modern agent-based theories for internet computation meet with philosophical logics of knowledge, belief, and intentions, social choice and theories of organization, and economic *game theory.* In 2005, I wrote a survey paper for the conference *Computing in Europe* entitled 'Computation as Conversation'. It shows how this mixture of computational, philosophical, game-theoretic, and social themes generates interesting parallels across disciplines, and new concrete questions for a joint theory of rational action. Theorems about computation give insights on what can be achieved through conversation, while conversely, conversational models are a powerful metaphor for computational design. My point is that all this is already happening: we just need to see things for what they are.

In fact, the story is potentially endless. One could easily generate other lists with similar points, looking at knowledge representation, general artificial intelligence, constraint satisfaction, algorithmics, complexity, security, learning theory, diagrammatic reasoning, or image processing. In each case, an initial practical setting induces fundamental theory whose themes, properly understood, far transcend computer science in a narrower sense.

What is missing? Well, I often wonder why so little of the above is known to a general audience. Most academics view informatics as just an auxiliary discipline, the handmaiden of implementation – and some computer scientists even pander to this subservient stance. As a final indignity: 'information science' means courses on libraries and how to order your filing systems. To change this, in a fashionable term, what is lacking is a good *Narrative*, a story line which makes it clear what has really been happening in the sciences of computation and information, and what cultural impact this has had, and still should have.

4. What do you consider the most neglected topics and /or contributions in late 20th century studies of computation and/or information?

So much is happening today that 'neglect' is not the first term that comes to mind! But the more exciting the landscape, the more new ridges to be climbed – so this question can always be answered. Here are a few themes on which I would like to see progress, if only for my own edification, going back to some issues touched upon in the preceding text.

One basic issue concerns the very notion of information. Is it really a coherent notion with consistent intuitions? Let us start with semantics. Current work on modal and epistemic logic concentrates on *information as range*. But there was also the situation-theoretic view of *information as correlation*. My Handbook chapter with Maricarmen Martinez tries to see the grand pattern behind both, and mergers are possible. But we still lack a consensus on the appropriate level of generality here – though I suspect it might lie with the general logics of *dependence* studied, e.g., by van Lambalgen, Hodges, and Väänänen.

But logic also has a combinatorial syntactic perspective on information, as the structure 'unpacked' by inference. This alternative view of information-as-elucidation is closer to logical proof and code-based computation, which come with their own elaborate theory. Again, there is no necessary conflict here: our Handbook chapter gives joint models of update and elucidation in specific settings – and just this year, there has been a bunch of papers merging this dynamic epistemic logic. But even so, I am not aware of one widely accepted paradigm combing the inferential sense of information with the semantic one. Over the years, there have been interesting attempts in the work of Carnap, Dunn, Hintikka,

Parikh, or Scott. But in my view, the price of abstract unification is still sometimes lack of exciting content. Even so, there is reason for optimism. Modern logic does have deep connections between proof and semantics. Just recall the celebrated result inaugurating the field, viz. Gödel's Completeness Theorem from 1929 showing that semantic validity and syntactic provability coincide for first-order predicate logic, the paradigm of modern logic.

Outside of logic, there is the more general interface between algorithmics and semantics, the two major prongs of the study of information and computation. There is interesting recent work of Abramsky, Adriaans, and others (cf. various chapters in the *Handbook of the Philosophy of Information*) on information flow in computation. Now, there need not be any unification here – maybe just a choice of 'life-style'. Occasionally, I get drawn into discussions (like with the Halting Problem, there is no decision method predicting beforehand if a conversation will turn out to be frustrating) with informatics colleagues telling me semantics has had its day, and that algorithmics should take over. Perhaps, but I am not yet ready to give up.

Further desiderata! I already mentioned the lack of Grand Narrative explaining the cultural role of informatics. One cause may be the lack of an agenda of *Grand Challenges*. In a pamphlet written with my Amsterdam colleagues Arnold Smeulders and Martin Stokhof in 1999, we tried the following seven, beyond the logic-oriented story I have told:

1. Why is cognition so efficient? (For instance, what goes on as you are grasping this interview?)

2. How do observation and internal reasoning combine in successful planning and acting?

3. How to integrate content from different carriers: for instance, both symbolic and graphic?

4. What is most efficient social organization for intelligent persons and machines?

5. Which conservation laws of complexity govern information processing?

6. How to integrate the Two Traditions: algorithmics, code, physical signal transmission, and semantic information from logic, linguistics, philosophy, and social sciences?

7. What are the computational mechanisms driving major cognitive activities like learning, and can we use them for practical social impact through our educational system?

I would definitely not plead for this particular list, but rather for an agenda where issues like these are stated and discussed – much in the spirit of Luciano Floridi's work.

Finally, here is another desideratum. I said that in principle, informatics has the same 'success formula' as modern physics, where fundamental research happens simultaneously with technological innovation. In the short term, this is also a problem, as the fast delights of engineering, applications that matter, and recognition may overwhelm the slow delights of insight in the light of eternity. Nevertheless, there is no necessary conflict – and there is no blame to be assigned. To the contrary, what we really have is an exciting Triangle with three vertices. There is empirical phenomena around us, fundamental theory behind this, but also a third activist stance, viz. the *design of new practices* inspired by theoretical ideas concerning information and computation. We already live in mixed societies populated partly by our biological off-spring and partly by virtual citizens put there by the information and computer sciences. These mixed societies raise fundamental issues again, such as understanding successful interactions between agents of very different abilities. You may want to recall, if you know your informatics culture, that the original *Turing Test* in AI was already of this kind. It did not ask if a computer can fully emulate a human being, but rather, whether in a group consisting of a computer and a human being, the latter could detect the type of the former. The third activist stance is itself worth pursuing – and an earlier-mentioned program like Parikh's 'social software' shows how surprising that can be. Informatics can change the world, and the distance between theory and practice is so small sometimes that this itself calls for reflection, if not participation.

5. What are the most important open problems concerning computation and/or information and what are the prospects of progress?

I have answered this question already under the preceding one. Let me just throw in two more things.

One concerns the *Handbook of the* Philosophy of Information, mentioned several times already. That book, to appear in 2008, brings together all major approaches to information in academia, and it draws basic philosophical lines – aiming for peaceful co-existence rather than grand unification. The authors represent both semantic and algorithmic traditions – with the latter all the way to quantitative Shannon information theory, Kolmogorov complexity, and probability theory. And here I will admit to a private perplexity when viewing all these chapters. To borrow a phrase, I would like to understand the 'unreasonable effectiveness' of quantitative information theories. To me, the idea that one can measure information flow one-dimensionally in terms of a number of bits, or some other measure, seems patently absurd—even when we admit that the number may be an average over many cases. But in reality, this quantitative approach is spectacularly success-ful, often much more so than anything produced in my world of logic and semantics. Why?

Finally, further mergers may be on the horizon. Is information and computation truly a natural frontier in Academia? Many top-ics on its agenda blend into empirical issues in *cognitive science*. Editing a recent 2007 issue of *"Topoi"* on 'Logic and Psychology' with Helen and Wilfrid Hodges, we found, often to our own sur-prise, how information, reasoning, computation, neural networks, learning, vision, and brain function form one natural conglom-erate, where biological function meets computational design. In particular, 'competing paradigms' from the last century are now meeting in surprising ways. Who would have thought that neural nets compute, much as default logics and event calculus in com-puter science, or that game theory would team up with linguistics and experimental psychology? Taking biological and psychological facts seriously is not uncontroversial in logical circles, but 'Infor-mation, Computation, and Cognition' may be the way to go.

16

Terry Winograd

Professor of Computer Science

Stanford University, USA

---

1. Why were you initially drawn to computational and/or informational issues?

I had a fascination with language and a love of mathematics. I was intrigued by the possibility that machines could be a model for human thought processes and that their ability to manipulate abstract symbols could be the basis for understanding language structure and use.

2. What example(s) from your work (or the work of others) best illustrates the fruitful use of a computational and/or informational approach for foundational researches and/or applications?

The most foundational work I have done is actually a critical re-examination of the relationship between symbolic processing and the communicative workings of ordinary human language. By stepping back and looking at the underlying assumptions of the computational/cognitive paradigm, it became clear that there were many ways in which it fell short of adequately capturing the phenomena of human understanding and language use. The result, as described in the book *Understanding Computers and Cognition* (Winograd and Flores, 1986) was a recognition that although there are many applications of computational models, they are at times misleading in offering easy but partial analogies with human language and symbol use. This was not superficially apparent, but required foundational philosophical analysis, drawn from phenomenology.

3. What is the proper role of computer science and/or information theory in relation to other disciplines, including other philosophical areas?

Computer science is a mix of disciplines. Some, e.g., computational complexity theory, being closer to mathematics, and others – including most of the work on hardware and software systems and applications – being more properly thought of as engineering. Very little of computer science is science in the traditional empirical mould of "unlocking the secrets of the universe." Given its breadth of perspectives, computer science has a wide diversity of roles with respect to other disciplines.

In philosophy, computers have served as a primary source of ideas and experiences that challenge long-held beliefs about the nature of mind and language. The existence of computer programs that can do many human-like activities gives us a new world of examples and Gedanken-experiments. Philosophers like Dennett have used this to great advantage in probing the presuppositions and understandings we bring from common sense. In psychology, although symbolic computational models have not proven to be generally applicable, they provide a point of reference and starting point from which to explore the more neurologically-inspired models of current research.

Of course, it goes without saying that computers and computation play a vital role in all of today's sciences, both as a model and as a tool. As one obvious example, biology has become deeply dependent on computing to deal with the vast amounts of information in the genome, the dynamics of complex molecules, and many more aspects. In a sense, we can see the 21st century ascendance of the biological sciences as a product of being able to deal with extreme complexity in a rigorous computational way.

4. What do you consider the most neglected topics and/or contributions in late 20th century studies of computation and/or information?

One of the areas that deserves more focus is the understanding of the process of Design. Simon's early work on this area (*The Sciences of the Artificial*) provides a starting point from within the cognitive paradigm. We need to move beyond that view and extend it to capture the richness of the design practices we see in the practice of technology development. We can see what people produce, but have few clear models of how they can do that effectively.

5. What are the most important open problems concerning computation and/or information and what are the prospects for progress?

The largest open problem is the relationship between computation, of the kind we understand from digital computers, and the informational activities of the human brain/mind. In the era that Haugeland calls "Good Old Fashioned AI" (GOFAI), theories such as Newell and Simon's physical symbol system hypothesis posited that there was a close necessary connection. As the research program based on that view has stagnated in the intervening several decades, there has been a simultaneous increase in the sophistication of our understanding of biological cognitive systems. Physiology, chemistry, and detailed function are all being decoded. Great progress in these directions is likely and will be facilitated by the ever-expanding capacity of computers and the increasing ability to observe and measure biological processes. The "decoding of thought" is a far-off but intriguing goal.

17

Stephen Wolfram

Founder and CEO

Wolfram Research Inc., USA

---

1. Why were you initially drawn to computational and/or informational issues?

At first, it was a very practical thing. I always believe in using the best tools. And in the early 1970s (when I was an early teenager), I happened to get interested in physics. And I realized that the best way to figure out some things I wanted to figure out in physics was to use a computer. So I learned how to do that.

In the years that followed, I became pretty good at using computers in practice to figure things out. And then, at the beginning of the 1980s, I decided to start building better tools for the kind of computing I wanted to do. And I realized that to do that I needed to understand more about the foundations of computation.

When I went on doing science, I then realized that I could apply what I'd learned about the foundations of computation. And the result was that I developed a new approach to science that's very fundamentally based on computational ideas.

2. What example(s) from your work (or the work of others) best illustrates the fruitful use of a computational and/or informational approach for foundational researches and/or applications?

I've now spent about twenty-five years applying computational ideas to questions in basic science. The single most fruitful concept has been exploring the computational universe of possible programs.

The exact sciences have always tended to use a fairly small set of models, mostly based on traditional mathematics. A key new concept from computation is to enumerate all possible programs – and potentially use them as models.

Studying the universe of possible simple programs defines a new kind of basic science. And what I've found is that that new kind of basic science is not only rich and fascinating in its own right – but is also immediately applicable. For what I've discovered is that in the universe of simple programs there are ones immediately relevant for understanding the natural world, for creating technology, and for creating all sorts of new forms and artefacts.

Learning about the computational universe also informs many old foundational questions in science and elsewhere. It shows us, at a basic level, why complexity is so easy for nature to produce, and so widespread. It shows us that there are fundamental computational limitations to traditional mathematical science. It gives us insight into how similar phenomena like intelligence are to natural processes. It shows us how special – and in many ways arbitrary – the formal systems like mathematics that we have built are.

3. What is the proper role of computer science and/or information science in relation to other disciplines?

Every discipline will inevitably become "computational" – and its methods and practice will become deeply infused with computation. I happen to have seen this personally over the past two decades as *Mathematica* and the computational capabilities it brings have spread through more and more fields.

Computation is crucial both to doing better what has been done before in other disciplines, and in defining fundamentally new approaches. In the past, mathematics and physics were the primary formal systems from which we took methods and language for other disciplines. Computation provides us a new – and very rich – underlying framework.

4. What do you consider the most neglected topics and/or contributions in late 20th century studies of computation and/or information?

Computer and information science have tended to define themselves in a rather engineering-based way – concentrating on creating and studying systems that perform particular specified tasks.

But there's a whole different approach that's much closer to natural science: to just investigate the computational universe of possible programs, and see what's out there.

One might have thought that most programs that one would encounter would not do anything very interesting. But the discovery that launched what I've done for the past quarter century is that that's not the case. Even remarkably simple programs – that one would quickly encounter in sampling programs from the computational universe – can show immensely rich and complex behavior.

There's a whole new kind of science that can be done by studying those programs.

5. What are the most important open problems concerning computation and/or information and what are the prospects for progress?

There's a lot still to discover about the computational universe. It's like many past explorations – whether of the flora and fauna of the earth, of the chemicals that can be created, or of the diversity of astronomical objects. We've learned enough to be able to do some basic classification, and we've been able to guess at some general principles. But there's a huge amount of detailed science to do in studying the computational universe.

There are a lot of important things that we might find in the computational universe. Perhaps we'll find an ultimate model for the physics of our actual, physical, universe. Perhaps we'll find the keys to many longstanding mysteries in science. Of one thing I am certain: in the computational universe there is a huge amount that we can mine for human purposes – for creating technology, or art, or other things that we as humans use.

For millennia, we have mined the natural world for objects and materials that we can use. But when it comes to procedures, forms or algorithms, we have tended to create them incrementally using traditional engineering methods. The computational universe provides a fantastically new rich source.

I and others have already created a growing body of technology derived from "mining" the computational universe. And this process will surely accelerate – so that in a few decades I expect that there will be more new technology obtained by mining the computational universe than by all the traditional methods put together.

References

Wolfram, S. 2002. *A New Kind of Science.* Champaign, Illinois: Wolfram Media, Inc.

http://www.stephenwolfram.com

About the Editor

Luciano Floridi (Laurea Rome "La Sapienza", MPhil and PhD Warwick, MA Oxon., www.philosophyofinformation.net) is Professor of Philosophy at the University of Hertfordshire, where he holds the Research Chair in Philosophy of Information in the School of Humanities, and Fellow of St Cross College, University of Oxford. He is President of the International Association for Philosophy and Computing (www.ia-cap.org).

Index